DEADLY RELATIONS

Today was my son Josh's first day of school, as an 8th grader. It was a day he was looking forward to. He had been idle too long. He needs the routine, and as I drove him to school I prayed that he would not encounter any trouble.

At school a couple of kids referred to him jokingly as John Doe. He buried the hurt and let it pass. Someone left a belt buckle with the initials "J. D." on his desk.

He took the bus home from school. As he neared home, a boy about his age came running up behind him shouting, "Are you Josh Nichols? Are you Josh Nichols?"

Josh said he turned to the boy, a little apprehensive because it was someone he didn't know and because of the way he had run up to him.

"Yeah, I'm Josh," he answered, not knowing what to expect.

"My name is John," the boy said coldly. "I'm from Oklahoma. My dad's a fireman in Oklahoma and his station had the windows blown out by the bomb your father set off. I could kill you."

Josh readied for a fight, but the boy just glared at him, then turned and walked away.

Victim #170 was getting a lesson in life.

By Blood Betrayed

My Life with Terry Nichols and Timothy McVeigh

Lana Padilla
with Ron Delpit

HarperPaperbacks
A Division of HarperCollinsPublishers

HarperPaperbacks *A Division of* HarperCollins*Publishers*
10 East 53rd Street, New York, N.Y. 10022

Cover photograph of Thomas James McVeigh and Terry Nichols by AP/Wide World Photos.
Cover photograph of the author Lana Padilla and Josh courtesy of Lana Padilla.

First printing: November 1995

Printed in the United States of America

HarperPaperbacks and colophon are trademarks of HarperCollins*Publishers*

❖ 10 9 8 7 6 5 4 3 2 1

For my mother, who never stopped praying for me, for Monica, who always believed in me, for my dad, who would have been proud of me, and for my Papeet, for whom I could do no wrong. Thank you all.

—R. D.

PREFACE

There were more than a few obstacles to the writing of this book, not the least of which were the FBI and other authorities who would just as soon have kept Josh and I as their own little secret.

There is also a great deal of emotion involved in telling a story that you have lived every day.

But because we lived it, and so far have survived it, I feel it is important to pass on our feelings and experiences not only to the public at large, but to those mothers and ex-wives who might one day face a similar fate.

I suppose, more than anything else, this entire ordeal has been a lesson in life. None of us are immune, and none of us are safe from having our lives turned upside down without warning.

The message it sends is something all of us must remember. A divorce may be final in the eyes of the court, but there is a good chance that if a former spouse is ever involved in, or accused of some heinous crime, that we will be tainted and painted with the same broad brush.

I am just an average, everyday worker. A single mother, like so many of you out there. And yet, I am in the news. People are calling to interview me and my son; they want to know our story, our thoughts. However it is not for anything we've done. It is only because I was married to Terry Lynn Nichols and Josh is his son.

What has happened to our lives is unbelievable. For all of those who said, "you ought to write a book," this is it.

I dedicate this to all the single mothers, and to the members of my family who have supported me throughout this entire nightmare.

By Blood
Betrayed

1

THE DRIVE FROM BOULDER HIGHWAY TO MCCARRAN
Airport was not usually annoying, but the traffic had
begun to thicken and was stop-and-go as the Las Vegas
afternoon rush hour approached.

A white-haired woman in an ages-old Cadillac with
huge tail fins cut across three lanes, forcing me to slow,
and I shot a hard glance at Terry.

"If you hadn't kept me waiting at the storage unit, we
could have avoided this traffic," I snapped. Truth was, I
had only waited fifteen minutes at AAAABCO Storage,
but the weather that day was warm and sticky and
enough to get me a bit irritated.

"Couldn't be helped," he said matter-of-factly. "After I
picked Josh up from school, he was starving. We stopped
to get him a hamburger and buzzed over as fast as we
could after that."

We had arranged to meet at the storage unit so Terry
could park his truck before his trip, but he and Josh
walked back to his space and spent another ten minutes
fooling around before finally announcing that they were
ready to go to the airport.

"Why did you need to go to the storage shed again?" I
asked, not really caring. "I thought you finished putting
away what you needed to store."

He didn't answer.

"These are the extra keys for the truck," he said, handing me a letter-size envelope. "Tim said he might need to borrow it," he continued. "He's having problems with his vehicle, so I told him I'd leave the keys and he could contact you if he came down from Kingman."

"*Tim*" was Tim McVeigh, a guy Terry'd met in the service and had become best buddies with despite McVeigh's being thirteen years younger. In the four years since their discharges, they had become almost inseparable, traveling and partnering up to buy and sell guns and other items at various gun shows.

It was November 22, 1994, and someone on the radio was reminding us that it was the day President Kennedy had been shot in 1963.

I squirmed in my seat, knowing that Terry probably remembered the date for another reason. It was the date his present wife's two-year-old son, Jason, had mysteriously died just a year before, suffocating in a plastic bag at their home in Kansas.

Tim McVeigh had discovered the body.

I looked at Terry Nichols out of the corner of my eye. He was my ex-husband, and I thought I knew him. I also thought the mention of November 22 might make him a little sad, but he sat mute, staring blankly out the window. I couldn't imagine what was going through his mind, because in recent years, despite the fairly close contact we maintained, Terry had become increasingly introverted and secretive.

He had spent the past two weeks staying at my house, sleeping on my couch and doing "guy" things with Josh like hunting, fishing, and occasionally going to Kingman to visit Tim and other ex-army buddies, but he had also walked around the house and slept with a loaded revolver tucked in the waist band of his jeans. It was just one of the changes in him that made me nervous.

The top was down on my convertible LeBaron and the wind in my hair and the sun on my face helped soothe my aggravation. I knew it wasn't the time or place to get bitchy with Terry, because our twelve-year-old son, Josh, was in the backseat, and he worshiped the ground his father walked on. A fight with Terry would only mean a confrontation with Josh later.

Terry was going to the Philippines, again, and silently I wondered how he could afford to keep shuttling back and forth between Cebu, Kansas, and Las Vegas. A one-way ticket cost about $1,200, and over the past four years Terry had traveled to the Philippines about four times a year, usually to see his young wife, Marife, a sort of mail-order bride he had married when she was seventeen. He had been introduced to her when she was fifteen, proposed to her by mail, and she had accepted.

She was still in school studying to be a physical therapist. They had a strange arrangement, what with her spending months at a time in the Philippines, then a few months in the States, then back in Cebu again.

I reasoned that this was why Terry visited the Philippines so often, but it wasn't. Sometimes he went when Marife was in Kansas. It didn't make sense, but I never asked why.

The first time he went I asked where he had gotten the money, and he said Tim had paid for his ticket. I found that a little odd, but I thought it was nice he had a friend who was willing to do this, and maybe Terry needed a vacation.

Now he was going to see his new wife, Marife, and I wasn't about to lecture him about being extravagant. No way I wanted to come off as the nagging or jealous ex-wife. Besides, despite the fact that Terry hadn't worked steadily in a couple of years, he had always been very frugal and would never have spent the money for the trip if he didn't think it necessary.

"Do they have Thanksgiving in the Philippines?" I asked, aiming to inject a lighter, clearly noncombative note into the conversation.

"No," he said dryly. "Think about it, Lana. Thanksgiving is a United States holiday." His tone was even, but he left no doubt he'd rather not talk or be bothered.

Other than McVeigh, I was probably Terry's only close friend. Some people said he didn't have friends because he was moody, but I wrote it off to him being a loner. He was never very social, and during the nine years we were married, our friends were almost all people I had met through my job in real estate.

For Josh's sake, I was sorry to see Terry go, but his presence as a houseguest for two weeks had put some additional strains on my marriage. My husband, Lee, wasn't exactly thrilled to have my ex sleeping on the couch, but he consented, in part because I told him how good it would be for Josh to see his dad, and because we didn't think Terry could afford a hotel.

And Terry was never underfoot. He and Josh were always out doing something, or off to Kingman to visit Tim or some of Terry's other army buddies.

We were nearing the airport and I had to concentrate on the signs. With all the construction and changes, McCarran was getting as complicated as big-city airports.

It was almost 4:30 when we pulled up to the curb in front of the Southwest terminal baggage area. Terry's flight didn't depart until 5:40, so he had plenty of time. He was going to fly to Los Angeles and have a short stopover before connecting to a Northwest flight to the Philippines.

"Thanks," he said.

"You're welcome," I replied, watching Terry get out of the car. I smiled to myself and thought, You really are a man of few words.

I followed him to the trunk and watched as he pulled his bags out and set them on the curb.

"That package is for you," he said, motioning to a neatly folded brown paper bag still on the floor of the trunk. "If I'm not back in sixty days, open it and follow the instructions."

My adrenaline was flowing, but before I could ask any questions he was walking away. He was dressed in khaki shorts and a pink button-down short-sleeved shirt, and all I could see was the back of his wavy brown hair as he lost himself in a crowd of other passengers trying to get their luggage checked.

A horn honked and I got back in the car.

Josh had positioned himself in the front seat and I checked to see that his seat belt was fastened before starting the car.

Suddenly he unfastened his belt and opened the door.

"I've got to give my dad a hug before he goes," he shouted. "I've got to." And like a big puppy in search of his master, he plodded down the sidewalk trailing Terry.

Twenty yards in front of me, I could see Josh bear hug his dad. He was almost as big as Terry, and he initiated the contact. Terry was shy about showing affection, but Josh wasn't about to let him get away without a last embrace.

A moment later a somber Josh slipped back heavily into the passenger seat, clicked his seat belt in place, and stared straight ahead. Trancelike. I had seen that look on his dad's face many times, and it made me think of the days and nights just prior to our divorce when Terry would sit in a chair on our farm in Decker, Michigan, and stare at nothing for hours on end.

It was five o'clock and the traffic was wicked. Two taxis and a tour bus zipped by and it was a minute or two before I noticed tears streaming down Josh's cheeks.

"What's the matter?" I asked softly.

"I'm never going to see my dad again," he said, sobbing. "I'm never going to see my dad again."

"Of course you will," I said reassuringly. "He's gone to the Philippines a lot of times. You know he always comes back."

"This time is different," he blurted through big tears.

And for the first time the fear that Josh might be right, and the thought of the mystery package and Terry's instructions to "open it if I'm not back in sixty days" all seemed like clear danger signals.

I said nothing else to Josh the rest of the way home. I didn't know what I could say. Was he simply overreacting or had Terry said something to trigger his fears?

I was concerned, but I was also determined not to make too much of it. Terry had gone and come back before, and I knew he had a sixty-day visa. Still, a certain part of me couldn't keep from thinking about the curious and suddenly worrisome little package in the trunk.

What was it? What, if anything, did it mean?

By the time we turned into our driveway, night had begun to drop its engulfing blanket, my anxieties were running at a sprinter's pace, and I was sure anyone within ten feet could hear the pounding of my heart.

I didn't take the bag out of the trunk, deciding to leave it there because no matter what it contained, I knew I didn't want to have to discuss it with my husband. Things were already very rocky between us, and if Terry had left me something personal, it might push Lee over the edge.

Josh didn't know about the package, so there was no chance of him bringing it up. In fact, for the rest of the evening he seemed to calm down. I figured he had just become overwrought knowing Terry would be gone for a couple of months.

Terry called from L.A. during his hour stopover, and it momentarily stopped my thoughts of impending doom.

"Had a little excitement at the airport after you left," he said, laughing.

"Oh. And what was that?" I asked, trying not to sound too inquisitive. With everything I had on my mind, I didn't have the nerve to talk to him about Josh's outburst or my own probably baseless worries.

"Airport security hassled me because I was carrying a couple of stun guns and they set off the metal detector. They even called the real cop on duty."

"What's so funny about that?"

"What's funny is, they ran me through the computer, and even though it showed I had a couple of outstanding traffic warrants, they didn't arrest me. They took the guns, but told me I could pick them up at baggage when I got to my destination."

He chuckled like a kid who had just put one over on his parents, said thanks again for the hospitality, and hung up.

What would possess him to think he could carry guns, even stun guns, on an airplane? I had no idea. All I knew for sure was that while on the surface he might seem normal, when you looked real close, Terry Lynn Nichols had some disturbingly strange habits.

And the fear wouldn't go away.

At midnight, I was lying in bed staring at the ceiling, praying that morning would hurry so I could be alone. Josh would head for school and Lee would be off to work. By 7:30, I could bring the package in and the minimystery would come to a screeching halt.

At 2:12 A.M., Josh came rumbling into our bedroom muttering something about a bad dream. I let him lie with us for a while, then, when I heard him breathing softly, I worked my way out of bed and into the kitchen to make coffee.

An hour later, I fell into an uneasy sleep on the couch, wishing for daylight.

It would be the first morning in two weeks that the phone didn't ring at seven o'clock with Tim McVeigh on the other end. During Terry's stay it was like a ritual. I'd answer and he'd say, "Hi, Lana. How are you? Is Terry around?" and I'd hand the phone to Terry, who always seemed to be expecting the call.

I never knew what they talked about, because once I handed Terry the phone, I'd retreat to my bedroom to get ready for work.

Today would be different.

No Terry. No Tim. No husband. No kids. No interruptions.

As soon as the house was empty, I nearly ran to the garage. I didn't even bother to put the door up, squeezing myself between the bumper and the inside back of the garage door to open the trunk.

There it sat, innocently staring back at me.

As badly as I wanted just to grab it and rip it open, something made me hold back. For a brief moment I froze. It was as if time stood still as I gazed at the bag, noticing how it was folded and wondering what was inside.

Despite all the wild scenarios I had envisioned, none would ever come close to the truth. There was no way I could have imagined how that little folded bag was going to change my life forever.

I picked it up carefully and took it inside. It wasn't heavy and it wasn't very thick, but I could feel something hard inside. I shook it and it rattled.

"Keys," I said out loud.

I set the bag on the dining-room table, still not sure I should open it. Terry had clearly ordered me not to open it for sixty days. He had only left yesterday.

"You're being silly," I told myself. "Do as you were told and leave well enough alone."

I left the package on the table and went into my room to get dressed for work. I felt better just knowing I had brought it inside. It wasn't necessary to open it. I'd take it with me to work and put it in the office safe.

Once upon a time you could drive from one end of Las Vegas to the other in about ten minutes.

Not so any more. Not since the building boom and new hotels like the MGM Grand and Mirage. Vegas had changed from Sin City to one of the country's most desirable places to live, and new residents were pouring in every day.

As a real-estate agent, I loved it, because many of the transplants came from California and had money in their pockets and stability in their eyes. They couldn't believe what they could get for their dollar. It was a win-win situation, which made it a lot better odds than they could get at the tables or the California Lottery.

It took nearly half an hour to get to my office, and I had changed my mind about opening the package at least five times during the drive. I may as well have played eeny-meeny.

Terry's little treasure bag stayed in the office safe less than half an hour.

In the end, I decided to go with my instincts. I was uneasy about his warning, and Josh's "I'll never see my dad again" kept echoing in my brain.

I went into the office conference room and closed the drapes.

A hard metal key chain with nearly a dozen keys in all shapes and sizes jangled as it slid out onto the conference-room table. I didn't recognize any of them.

I pushed the keys aside and pulled the papers out of the envelope.

There was a sealed letter addressed to Tim McVeigh's sister, Jennifer, Terry's life-insurance policy with a note that he had changed his beneficiary from me to Marife on

November 7, and two handwritten lists of things for me to "Read and Do Immediately." There was also a reference to a storage unit rented under the alias of Ted Parker, also on November 7. (See page 219)

I was astonished. Even though I just scanned the Read and Do list, it was obvious Terry had no intention of coming back. It read like a last will and testament, right down to his notation that "all items in storage are for Joshua. The 'round' items are his when he turns twenty-one, all else now."

He also referred to something he had hidden in my house, explaining how he had taped a plastic bag behind the utensil drawer in my kitchen.

"All items in plastic bag are to be sent to Marife, for Nicole, if for any reason my life insurance doesn't pay her. Otherwise, half goes to Josh and half to Marife." Nicole was Terry's two-year-old daughter by Marife and I knew how protective he was of her.

Inside the letter to Jennifer was another stamped and sealed envelope, this one addressed to Tim McVeigh.

The carefully printed note to Tim was both startling and confusing, and it wasn't until months later, after examining it for weeks, that the FBI was able to decode the hidden messages.

Even though I didn't understand what Terry was trying to say, phrases such as "You're on your own now. Go for it!" and "This letter is written for the purpose of my death" were enough to send icy lasers shooting up my spine.

It was a suicide note. A damn suicide note.

Terry was going to kill himself!

The two weeks he'd spent with Josh were just his way of saying good-bye.

I hated him. I hated him for what he was going to do to Josh and for the trauma his son would have to live with the rest of his life.

Tears were streaming down my face, but I was so engrossed in the material in front of me I didn't notice until they stained one of the pages of Terry's notes.

I copied the combination to the storage lock, gathered up the pages, put them back in the grocery bag, and returned them to the office safe. There was nothing else I could do. Terry was in the Philippines and I had no way to reach him, or know if he was still alive.

Next, I had to find out what was hidden at my house and what in God's name he had left in the storage unit. However, I wanted to do it without alarming Josh or anyone else in the family. I wasn't ready to subject Josh to any unnecessary pain, so I decided to wait until he left to visit his grandparents over Christmas vacation before exploring any further.

Two agonizing weeks passed before the perfect time arose.

It was December 15. Josh was in Michigan and my husband was at work. I recruited my older son Barry to assist me, primarily because I was afraid to find whatever it was I was going to find alone.

We worked quickly and silently, focusing on the kitchen-utensil drawer first. We removed the drawer from the runners and pushed down on two small levers Terry had installed at the back of the cabinet.

Barry stretched his arm to the back and detached a plastic Ziploc bag crammed with cash, all in twenties and hundreds.

We were too shocked to do anything but stare at each other. I spread the money out on the table and counted it.

"Twenty thousand dollars," I exclaimed sarcastically. "And I thought Terry was poverty-stricken. Where the hell did he get that much money?"

The money convinced me he was now dead and had sold his guns or other equipment to provide some sort of support fund for his kids, Josh and Nicole.

AAAABCO storage was our next stop. Barry drove. He was twenty-three and my oldest son. We had been through some tough times, surviving his bouts with drugs and alcohol and my four marriages, yet somehow still managed to bond.

A tense quietness took hold as Barry and I walked apprehensively down the dimly lit corridor toward unit Q106. We didn't even look at one another.

Barry fumbled with the lock for a moment, then spun the tumbler.

"Thirty-nine," I half whispered, suddenly no longer sure I wanted to know what was inside.

In seconds the lock opened. Barry rolled up the door and pulled the string on the overhead light.

Neither of us knew what to say.

The survivalist gear was no surprise. Terry had told me he was storing his tent and fishing gear.

But there were wigs, masks, panty hose, freeze-dried food, and various gold coins (obviously the "*round*" objects for Josh), along with gold bars and silver bullion stacked neatly in boxes. There were also some small green stones that appeared to be jade. I estimated at least $60,000 street value in precious metals!

"I wonder what these are for," Barry said alarmingly. He was holding up a circular key ring with at least twenty-five keys. Many of them appeared to be to safety-deposit boxes or public storage lockers, and I wondered what additional secrets Terry could possibly be hiding, and why?

The rest of the month was a blur. Christmas came and went and January brought rain and cold to the first month of 1995. My heart was already cold. I hadn't heard a word from or about Terry. My attempts to contact him in the Philippines were futile.

On January 14 he called.

"I'll be back in Las Vegas day after tomorrow," he said. "I'm not sure exactly what time because international flights are sometimes delayed. I'll call you when I get to the Vegas airport."

The phone wasn't the way to tell him I'd opened his package or rummaged through his storage unit. I had a thousand questions, all of which I was afraid to learn the answers to.

Terry arrived shortly after 11:00 P.M. on a Thursday. I picked him up and drove him directly to the Boulder storage facility to get his truck. We hardly spoke and he didn't seem to notice my concern.

"Is it okay if I get the truck and crash on your couch until tomorrow?" he asked. "I'll be heading back to Kansas then."

"I suppose."

I was already in bed by the time he got to the house. I had left the front door open. It wasn't until the next morning that we spoke.

"Where's the package?"

"I opened it," I stated boldly, the anger I'd been holding in for more than a month surfacing.

"Why?" He was seething. "You betrayed my trust. I told you not to open it for sixty days."

"Because I was frightened. I thought something terrible had happened to you. I thought you were dead. And where did you get all that money?" I wasn't afraid anymore. Maybe I was even looking for a fight.

"Where's the money?"

I went into my bedroom and returned with an envelope.

"There's fifteen thousand dollars in there," I challenged. "I'm keeping the other five thousand for Josh. For support."

"You can't do that, Lana. I need that money." He wasn't screaming, but his voice was loud and the veins in his neck were bulging.

The shrill ring of the phone momentarily interrupted the verbal onslaught.

It was Tim McVeigh.

The conversation was brief.

When he hung up, Terry had a reason to be insistent.

"Lana, I've gotta have that money. Tim needs to borrow it." His tone was just as firm, but less boisterous.

"You'd lend it to Tim and not give it to your son?" I said indignantly. "I don't think so."

Eventually we compromised. I returned $2,000 and put the other $3,000 away for Josh.

A day later Terry cleared out his storage unit, packed up, and disappeared.

He never asked about the letters in the package and I didn't mention them, but intuition told me they were important. I made copies and tucked them away in the rear of the office safe.

What I saw in the storage shed, and the man Terry Nichols had become worried me. Sometimes you just have a feeling that something bad is going to happen.

I had that feeling.

On April 21, I found out why.

That was the day the FBI and I became formally acquainted. They put in a call to me at home at 8:30 A.M., but I had already left for work. My son gave them the office number to Esquire Realty and they called before I got there.

When I arrived, the realtor who had taken the call raised an eyebrow as she handed me a message saying the FBI wanted to talk to me.

"What'd you do, Lana, rob a bank?" she said with a wink.

I returned their call and Dan Walters asked if he and another agent could come by and talk to me for a few minutes.

"Sure. I'll be in the office all morning," I offered.

I was pretty sure what it was about.

A few years back, during the period when my marriage to Terry was in its final stages, I won a weekend getaway to Las Vegas in a contest sponsored by my insurance office.

Terry was moody and pouty and expressed no interest in going, so I decided to go alone. On the trip I met and had a brief fling with a flashy Sicilian, who turned out to be a small-time con man. We had an exciting and erotic weekend, but his later scams eventually earned him an expense-free stay in a federal institution. At one point he was transferred to a Michigan prison and I visited him a few times, but I knew he and I were going nowhere. I couldn't see myself leaving Terry and winding up with an ex-con. I had often been stupid about men, but this wasn't going to be one of those times.

When I left Michigan for Vegas, he was ticked at me for giving up on him and "breaking up our relationship." I heard from a friend that he had broken parole and was threatening to come west to pay me a visit. I figured this was what the feds were coming to warn me about.

Little did I know.

Less than fifteen minutes later Agents Alan Gough and Dan Walters appeared at the office.

They asked if there was a place we could talk privately and I ushered them into the same conference room where I had originally opened Terry's package. When I was seated they laid out a couple of black pencil sketches and asked if I recognized the men in the pictures.

"That's Tim McVeigh," I responded, pointing to the picture on the left. "And that's Terry. Why do you want to know? What did they do?"

"They're suspects in the Oklahoma City bombing," the agent said soberly.

The blast at the Alfred P. Murrah Federal Building in Oklahoma City had happened two days before and 1,800 miles away, but the moment I saw those pictures, a bomb exploded in the center of my heart. . . .

2

"DO YOU KNOW WHERE TERRY IS RIGHT NOW?"

Alan Gough was speaking softly, almost in measured tones, but there was an urgency in his voice.

He was a nice-looking man, in his mid forties with slightly graying hair and a round, pleasant face. He had turned the heads of a couple of female sales agents when he walked into my office earlier and I could see why. At five-eight and about 160 pounds, he appeared to be in good shape, and his intense blue eyes commanded your attention.

"I assume he's at home," I answered quickly. "I spoke to him earlier this morning."

"You spoke to him today?" the two agents said almost in unison.

"I called him early this morning, around seven-thirty Las Vegas time. We spoke for about ten minutes. I had to talk to him about our son, Josh." They were shocked I had spoken to Terry so recently. Josh had come home from Kansas and told my older son Barry that Terry had said I'd stolen $3,000 of the money he had left with me for safe-keeping while he was in the Philippines. I did not volunteer what our conversation was about, and didn't think it necessary to tell them I was angry at Terry for saying this and spent most of the time chewing him about it.

Terry had actually stooped to claiming he could have gotten new eyeglasses if I hadn't taken the money. It was the second time in a week I wound up having words with him about the money.

The first day Josh arrived in Kansas, I called to be sure he had gotten in safely and Terry brought it up. It was as if he wanted to pick a fight.

"You said you were going to use that money for Josh," he snapped, "so I want to see a bank receipt. Show me it was deposited in an account in his name and it's going to go for him."

"I've used that much for him in the past two years and you haven't contributed a dime," I spat right back at him. He'd been a no-account nomad practically living out of his truck and receiving mail at a post office box for the past year and a half, and he had the nerve to rag on me.

"Have you had any other contact with Terry?" one of the agents asked, seeming to accept my explanation for the first call to Terry without further detail. I was sitting at the conference table lost in thoughts that made no sense.

Terry couldn't have done this. I just spoke to him. He would have said something. He sounded normal even though he was a bit rushed. I figured he just wanted to get off the phone because I was bitching at him. Besides, what possible reason could he have for blowing up a darn building and killing innocent people?

"Mrs. Padilla . . ." Agent Walters's voice shook me back to the present. I hadn't answered the question. I hadn't replied because another thought about the original argument with Terry came rushing back.

"You know, Lana, I could make your life miserable," he had said back in November when I refused to give him back the money.

"What are you going to do, Terry, shoot me?" I wasn't

afraid of him, but maybe I should have been. Maybe there was a dark side to him that I wasn't aware of, or had paid no attention to.

Dan Walters was at least four inches taller than his partner, and a number of years younger, with schoolboy good looks and wavy brown hair, but he was just as persistent.

"We speak whenever he calls to talk to Josh," I explained, putting the old thoughts away. "In the past week I've talked to him a couple of times because Josh was visiting him in Herington over the Easter break. He got back late Monday night, actually Tuesday morning around 1 A.M."

It also wasn't necessary to tell them that he had been uncomfortable, and that Marife was standing at his side, and that they had just had a fight —over me, and whether he was still in love with me.

Then, almost as an afterthought, I added, "He left some papers with me that you may want to see. I can't make heads or tails out of them." I don't know how, at that moment, I remembered the package I had tucked away in the office safe four months earlier, or why I volunteered to retrieve it, but I did. Perhaps it was fear, or more accurately the desire to cooperate in any way I could so they didn't think I was involved or trying to hide anything.

This has turned out to be one of the most meaningful decisions of my life and I relive it a thousand times every day, because while the letters undeniably linked Terry and Tim, and hinted in a coded way of some surreptitious plan or plot, the fact that I had been entrusted with them showed Terry's complete confidence that I could be counted on to do whatever he asked.

"I trust you more than anyone in the U.S." is the line that caught the attention of authorities, who later wondered aloud if there might be a hidden meaning, and maybe

Terry Nichols had foreign ties he might have trusted more.

I felt as if I were in a trance as I wobbled a bit unsteadily to the office safe. It took me a minute or so to locate the letters and I felt like a character out of The Stepford Wives as I moved to the Xerox machine to copy them.

I was nervous, which might also explain why I was being overly cooperative. Also a bit frightened. But I had no reason to be. I hadn't done anything.

The men looked over the letters without changing expression.

"Do you mind if we take these?" Gough asked politely.

Walters asked if there was a phone he could use privately and left to make a call from one of the unused office cubicles. He returned a minute or two later.

"Is it possible you could come down to the FBI office with us for some additional questions, Mrs. Padilla?" It was Walters speaking and I knew I was hearing the result of his phone call.

"Shouldn't take too long," Gough chimed in reassuringly. Their smooth teamwork left me no room to decline.

I was still stunned and slightly overwhelmed by it all as I gathered up my purse and briefcase and took a quick look around my office to see if I was forgetting anything.

"I should be back in a couple of hours," I called to my partner, Kay Bignotti, as I headed for the door, my ever-present Diet Pepsi in hand. It was 10:30 in the morning.

"If I have any calls, tell them I'll return messages in the afternoon."

None of us could have dreamed it would be fifty-four days before I'd set foot in the office again, and when I did, my life would have changed completely.

I rode to the FBI offices on Charleston Boulevard with Alan Gough, having forgotten in all the confusion that I had been dropped off at the office by a friend who was going to have my car serviced.

It was late April, the tail end of the rainy season in Vegas, and a light mist splashed over the windshield as Agent Gough turned the plain-looking sand-colored four-door Plymouth onto the eastbound Interstate 95 on-ramp.

There was very little traffic and the drive took only about twelve minutes, but it seemed longer because we hardly spoke. I didn't know if it was appropriate for me to ask him about the case, and I was fairly certain he wouldn't tell me anyway.

"The rain is nice," I said, not knowing what else to say.

"We need more of it."

"Have you lived here long?" I was forcing myself to make conversation with this man who was driving me to who knew what.

"About eleven years."

"Well, if you ever need to buy a house, give me a call." I handed him one of my business cards and he smiled.

"Just might do that."

I stared out the rain-spattered passenger window and braced myself for what I hoped would be a brief and non-stressful question-and-answer period.

The bombing had taken me as much by surprise as everyone else in the country.

I was on my way to work two days earlier when I heard a radio report that a bomb had exploded inside a building in Oklahoma City. My first reaction was shock, but as the newsperson continued with details, I felt sick to my stomach. How could anyone do anything so unspeakable?

By the time I reached my office, everyone was talking about it. I commiserated with my coworkers while I poured my morning coffee, then tried to put it all out of my head and get ready for my first appointment.

That was then. This was now, and Gough was turning off Charleston into the FBI parking lot.

"Please stay in the car. I'll come around and get your door," he said in a monotone.

In the mirror I could see him scanning the parking area as he moved to open my door. I wondered if he carried a gun.

The FBI offices were located on the third floor and Agent Gough offered me a choice of transportation.

"Stairs or elevator?"

"I don't mind the stairs," I said gamely. "I can use the exercise."

"So can I."

Within minutes after walking up the three flights of stairs, I was introduced to Las Vegas FBI Director Randy Prillaman. He was tall, around six-two, I guessed, and even though his manner remained soothing, he skipped the small talk.

He showed me into his office, with Agent Gough just a step behind, helped me into a dark brown leather sofa, and got right to business.

"We need you to give us some information about Terry," he began. "Mostly background, and whatever you can recall that relates to those letters you had. I'm sure anything you can tell us will be helpful in trying to get to the bottom of what happened and who did it."

His mention of the letters confirmed my suspicion that Agent Walters had called him from my office and explained the package I was holding.

"Why do you think Terry is part of the bombing?" I wanted to know.

"We don't know that he is, Mrs. Padilla," Prillaman answered. "We just need to get more information so we can try and get a clearer picture. The more information we have, the better chance we have of eliminating certain people as suspects."

He was very glib and made me feel as if I had sinned and everything would be all right as soon as I cleansed myself through confession.

"I'd like you to talk with Agent Gough, Mrs. Padilla. By the way, is it pronounced Padill-uh or Padee-a?"

"Padee-a, but it's okay for you to call me Lana."

"Thank you, Mrs. Padilla. As I was saying, I'll leave you here with Agent Gough and he'll run through some questions with you. This is all informal, so just relax and answer as best you can. If you don't understand something he asks, or can't remember, just tell him that. We'd rather not have you guess."

The director gone, Gough wasted no time in going after what he wanted. His method of questioning was subtle but direct, and pretty much paralleled the easygoing personality I had perceived in him. Nonetheless his questions came in a torrent.

"Do you think Terry could be dangerous?" he began, interpreting my silence as permission to proceed. "Does he have or keep a lot of guns at his home?"

"I'm not sure what you mean by 'dangerous,'" I replied, not trying to be evasive.

"Is he violent? Does he have a temper?"

The phone buzzed before I could answer and Gough excused himself for a moment. He returned with a slightly more relaxed way of proceeding.

"You spoke to Terry this morning. Is that correct?"

I nodded. "Just for a few minutes."

"Would you be willing to call him again if we need you to?"

"Yes, I guess so, if you want me to," I stammered.

"I'm not sure if it's going to be necessary, but we would like to put you on the phone with a hostage coordinator in Kansas. He's going to ask you some questions. Please try and answer them as honestly as you can."

My heart was pounding so hard I could hear it in my

ears. The building was huge, these people were important. What they were talking to me about was incredibly serious and what the hell was I doing here? In the middle of it all.

Prillaman reappeared, bringing a new circumstance for me to worry about.

"We'll want to bring the rest of your family in, just to be sure they're safe," the director said as we walked toward the room where the phone was waiting with the hostage coordinator on the other end.

"Josh is at school. Barry's at home, and Troy's at work. At Apple Plastics." All of it just spilled out, seemingly without any thought process.

"Why don't you call Josh's school first," Prillaman suggested, and picked up a phone on the next desk.

I got the principal at Cannon Middle School on the line, but I began to babble. Suddenly I couldn't put a sentence together.

"Here, you talk to him," I said in frustration, and handed the phone to Prillaman.

Eventually someone arranged for the friend with my car to pick Josh up within the hour, deciding that would be less conspicuous than having him brought in by FBI agents without explanation.

"We'll send a car to your house to pick up Barry. You can call Troy at work and arrange for him to come in after his shift. Josh is the one we're most concerned with right now."

I heard "Josh . . . most concerned with . . ." and I came unglued.

"Josh didn't do anything, did he?" I was frantic. I had never even considered that Josh might be involved. Oh God, I prayed, please tell me he didn't have anything to do with the bombing! I knew my voice had cracked and risen three octaves, but I temporarily lost control.

"Easy, Lana." It was Randy Prillaman speaking. "Let's

not jump to conclusions. No one has even suggested that Josh might be involved, or know anything about all of this. It's our job to be cautious, and to protect you and your family."

His repeated assurances eased my concerns a bit, but I knew something he didn't know yet. Josh not only worshiped his father, he did whatever his father asked him to do, and he did not share these things with me unless he felt it necessary to do so.

I called Barry and Troy and briefly explained what was happening. It was obvious their presence was not absolutely necessary, probably because they weren't Terry's kids. Their surname was Osentowski. Their father was a louse who treated me badly until I walked out on him, but he had never done anything to get him or me hauled into FBI headquarters.

The family arrangements made, Randy Prillaman turned me over to Alan Gough again and we proceeded into yet another office where an agent waited with a phone receiver in hand.

The hostage coordinator, who could have been a cop, a psychologist, or both, asked the kind of questions needed to compile a psychological profile of Terry.

Was he moody? Was he angry or prone to violence? What was his religious preference?

"Atheist, I guess. He said he didn't believe in anything."

Was he depressed or despondent? What were his interests? Was he having any marital difficulties? Was he happy? How did he feel about the government?

I answered everything as completely as I could, but many of the questions were complex. Terry was an intelligent man, but he wasn't very forthcoming in conversation. He had gone to college with the intention of being a doctor but had dropped out after a year when his mother called and asked him to come back to the farm to help with the crops. He didn't talk about that much, and God knows he'd never blame his mother for anything, but I knew it bothered him. Leaving school kind of got him off-track. I always had the feeling he would like to have made more of himself, and resented not having finished. But he didn't brood about it.

He was handy at fixing things, an excellent carpenter, and quite adept at ferreting out solid investments in penny stocks and charting the stock market. He had even passed a very difficult test and earned a securities license with only a modicum of study and preparation.

Terry wasn't moody, but he did seem confused and bored a lot of times, as if he knew he was capable of better things. When he was angry he'd keep it inside, although from time to time he did express his dissatisfaction with the government.

I knew he had renounced his American citizenship sometime after we'd split, declaring himself some sort of resident nonalien, which I didn't understand, but figured, what the hell. To each his own. As long as it didn't affect me. Or Josh.

Since our divorce, I'd heard about Terry doing a number of weird things. Nothing dangerous, but definitely strange. There was something about him rebelling against a credit-card company after running up thousands of dollars in charges, and I'd heard he had a sticker or some crazy slogan stamped on his driver's license claiming the roads belonged to all men and not the government or state and that he wasn't required to pay taxes.

I had been on the phone with the hostage coordinator about twenty minutes when another agent entered and whispered something I couldn't hear into Gough's ear. Gough nodded.

"It's okay now," he said calmly, and I shot him a puzzled look. "Terry's turned himself in to the authorities in

Kansas," he explained. "We won't need the hostage people anymore."

Nor would they need the SWAT team or the platoon of armed and bulletproof-vested Alcohol, Tobacco and Firearms agents we later saw on TV, who were prepared to surround and storm Terry's house if necessary.

It was about 12:40 in the afternoon and a wave of relief began to sweep through me. It was over. What an ordeal. We could go home now and get back to our lives.

"Your son is here. In the front office," an agent informed me. And I felt relieved. Even motherly. I said thank you, but inside I wanted to run to Josh and throw my arms around him. I wanted everything to be okay and for it all to go away, but it wouldn't.

My friend hadn't given Josh much background. Only that I had been taken to FBI headquarters for questioning, and that it had something to do with his dad.

Josh's bright blue eyes said it all as I walked toward him. They were burning with curiosity.

I answered his questions before he could ask.

"They think your dad had something to do with the Oklahoma bombing," I said, looking at him squarely. I didn't believe in coddling kids. Loving them yes, but not protecting them from the truth. He was going to find out all the details anyway.

The TV had been on since I arrived, but because of the questioning, I hadn't really been able to follow what was being said. A couple times I had seen pictures of Terry and Tim on the screen when I looked up, but I couldn't hear the sound. Now Josh and I huddled close together on the sofa, our eyes transfixed on the box sitting on the credenza across from Director Prillaman's desk, bringing us the constant news and reports from Oklahoma City and Kansas.

Terry had always referred to the TV as a "one-eyed mindsucker" and Josh had picked up the terminology. He used it like a little catchphrase, I suppose because it reminded him of Terry.

Outside the director's office a cluster of agents, maybe six or seven, all seemed to have a phone to their ear. They were working at a long conference table that had ten or twelve phones. In a way it reminded me of a telemarketing boiler room. Every so often they'd look up from the phone to watch as CNN and Headline News announced fresh news about the bombing and Terry's surrender. They flashed updates every few minutes giving some new detail about Terry's life. I wondered how they had gotten so much information so quickly.

"Nichols is a former army buddy of suspected bomber Tim McVeigh. . . ."

"Sources say Nichols, forty, became friends with Tim McVeigh in the army when both were stationed at Fort Riley, Kansas. . . ."

"Nichols, who joined the army at the late age of thirty-three, was granted a hardship discharge in 1989. No details are available about why he was discharged. . . ."

"It has been reported that Nichols renounced his American citizenship four years ago, declaring himself a 'resident nonalien'. . . ."

"So far, McVeigh and Nichols are the only persons arrested in connection with the bombing that has killed scores of people in the Alfred P. Murrah Federal Building in Oklahoma City. . . ."

"Neighbors of the Kansas man arrested today say Terry Nichols was a quiet man who kept to himself and minded his own business. . . ."

"The forty-year-old Nichols lived briefly in Las Vegas, and was once married to Las Vegas realtor Lana Padilla. The couple has a twelve-year-old son, Josh. . . ."

There it was. Our names were on the news. Did somebody suspect us? Did they think we had something to do with it?

Within minutes of my name being mentioned on TV, my cellular started ringing. Someone named Bob from *The New York Times* wanted a comment about Terry's surrender. And did I know if he did the bombing for revenge and was he part of a militia group?

"I don't know anything," I sobbed into the phone, and hung up.

Immediately, it rang again.

"Mrs. Padilla? This is Helen with Channel Eight news."

I didn't wait for her questions. I pressed "end" and turned off the phone.

"I think we ought to take this," said Prillaman, reaching for the little instrument that was so vital to my business. "We'll get you hooked up with a new number right away."

Tears were running down my cheeks and I didn't know why. I was crying for no reason and couldn't stop.

It felt odd seeing Terry's picture on television, especially since he had always been such a shy, introverted person.

"There's our old house," Josh said in a voice louder than he realized.

One of the stations was showing a picture of the Decker, Michigan, farmhouse we had lived in for a couple of years when I was married to Terry. Seeing it on TV brought back memories.

Josh had been born in that house, and despite the fact that we shared it with Terry's brother, James, it had never seemed cramped. Perhaps because it was a solidly built, rambling three-story ranch house with five bedrooms and lots of space.

But this time the news bulletin wasn't about Terry. It was about James. Agents had the farmhouse surrounded and we could see from the live camera shots that they had their weapons drawn.

"Armed federal and state authorities converged on a Michigan home today in search of evidence in the bloody bombing in Oklahoma," the announcer proclaimed, raising his voice to get the right inflection.

"Sanilac County Sheriff Virgel Strickler said agents searched a farmhouse and surrounding buildings belonging to James Nichols in Decker, Michigan, a quiet rural community about eighty-five miles north of Detroit.

"The FBI told sheriffs and other local officials that agents had received information that evidence linked to the Oklahoma bombing might be found on the Decker property. Sheriff Strickler said the homeowner, James Nichols, arrived shortly after investigators did, and was served with a search warrant."

A later report indicated that whoever rented the Ryder truck believed to have been used in the Oklahoma City bombing allegedly used James Nichols's address, 3616 North Van Dyke Road in Decker.

Oh great. The whole darn family was involved! Did James get Terry into this mess, or was it Tim? Or were they all involved? My imagination was running amok. Maybe Terry wasn't involved. Maybe they were really looking for James and Terry was only implicated because he was James's brother and had once lived at that address.

Josh looked at me with a shocked and pained expression. I didn't have any answers.

"Let's go in here so we can talk," said Prillaman, intruding on my thoughts as he led me away from Josh and into an empty office.

It was two in the afternoon. I had been there three hours and it seemed like four days.

Agent Debbie Calhoun got Josh a soda and the two of them settled into Prillaman's office.

"He'll be fine," Prillaman said, sensing my concern. "Debbie's excellent with kids." Just the way he said it made me feel better. Despite my earlier discomfort about his manner, Prillaman impressed me as a very caring man and one who was sympathetic to our position.

Almost on cue Alan Gough materialized at the door of the office where Prillaman had transferred.

"You guys moved around on me," Gough joked.

"Her son Josh is here now and Debbie's interviewing him in my office. You and Lana can work in here, and I'll come by and check on you in a little bit." Then, addressing me: "Lana, Alan will need to finish interviewing you. If you have any problems or need anything, ask for me."

They wanted to know everything, seemingly asking anything that came to mind in connection with my relationship with Terry.

Why did he join the army? What was the state of our marriage at the time? Did he like children? Did I know any of his "other" friends?

No, I didn't, because Terry didn't have many friends. When we were married, I was his closest friend. Friends we made were my friends, through business. He wanted to be friends with his brother, James, but they always seemed to end up in squabbles, because James tried to boss Terry around.

After the army, Tim became his closest friend.

Terry didn't even have any old girlfriends hanging around. Near as I could tell, he hadn't dated much before meeting me, and he was considered pretty much of a dud when it came to women. Which isn't necessarily true, because our sex life was pretty good. I think he just didn't like all the formality of dating and asking a girl out and building a relationship.

Some of the things Gough asked seemed so remote, I couldn't see any way the answers could be useful. Occasionally, there was a question about McVeigh, but not many.

Terry was definitely the main event of the day.

And at every silent moment I kept thinking this had to be all one big mistake. I knew Josh was okay, but at that moment I wanted him near me, just to hold him for comfort. And I wanted to get back to the television so I could hear and see what was going on.

Gough jotted down my answers at a furious pace, often asking me to repeat things, and I wondered why he didn't use a tape recorder. But none of the agents did. They later transferred their notes to what they called "302s," which is FBI jargon for interrogation reports.

By 2:30 Barry had been brought in, after having the FBI agents wait while he took a shower. That was Barry. Never one to be rushed. Shortly after his arrival, Troy showed up, and within minutes they had us each in separate rooms, being questioned by different agents.

News of James's arrest on explosives charges filtered in during the questioning, throwing no more light on what was going on, just making it all the more bizarre. He and Terry had been taken into custody within hours of each other. Now they were both in jail, Terry in Kansas and James in Michigan. Every minute it was becoming more and more of a nightmare.

The interviews with Barry and Troy were fairly brief, and we were able to take a break around 4:15. Barry and Troy had lived with Terry and Josh and me in Michigan but that was back in the late eighties so they didn't have a lot to add to the quickly thickening file the agents were assembling on Terry.

On a number of occasions, when a particular answer struck a nerve, Agent Gough would excuse himself and step into another room to make a call. I figured he was buzzing Prillaman, calling a higher-up in Washington, or someone in Kansas to relay the information and see how it stacked up against what, if anything, Terry was saying.

He was patient, and he was thorough, and never did he adopt an adversarial tone or demeanor. But none was necessary, because I was cooperating fully and telling them everything I knew.

When we got around to the subject of Josh's just-concluded week in Kansas with his dad, I could sense the tension.

"You know, it's odd," I said to Gough. "At first, Terry wasn't even sure he wanted Josh to come visit during Easter break. He made some lame excuse about having to go and do some gun shows and there not being enough room in his truck for Josh. He said with his wife, Marife, their daughter, Nicole, himself, and the merchandise, it was going to be awfully crowded.

"But I pushed him. I wanted Josh to go and see his dad, and I needed the break, too. Josh had been getting a little difficult to handle and I felt two weeks with his dad would be a nice vacation for us both.

"Terry relented and said Josh could come, but only for a week. Then, a day or two before Josh was scheduled to return, Terry called and asked if he could stay a couple extra days. Ordinarily I would have said yes, because his dad is so far away and because Josh had been having a really hard time at school in the weeks before he left. But something inside me made me say no. I still don't know why. Call it a mother's intuition. Still, if I hadn't pushed so hard for Josh to go in the first place, maybe none of this would have happened." I tried to fight back the tears but couldn't.

"Don't beat yourself up, or play what-if," Gough said, handing me a tissue to dry my weepy eyes. "You're doing just fine, Mrs. Padilla. Why don't we take a break so you can stretch your legs and catch your breath?"

"I'm all right," I mumbled, "but I would like to call my dad and my sister if I could. If they've seen any of this on television, they're probably pretty worried about us. I'd like to let them know we're okay."

"You can use this phone," he said, and got up from the

desk. "Just punch an open line and dial direct." He smiled and disappeared through the door.

I hadn't seen Josh in about forty-five minutes, not since he'd left with the female agent, but I assumed he was okay. I hope they're feeding him and not caning him, I thought, trying to inject a bit of humor to calm myself down. It didn't work. I was really in a fog, not knowing what I should or shouldn't do.

My dad answered on the first ring. He owned a huge combination crop-and-dairy farm in the thumb area of Michigan, and even though he was near seventy, he was still an active farmer. The fact that he was in the house and not in the field told me he knew what was happening.

"What the heck's going on, Lana?" he asked after I assured him Josh and I were okay.

"I don't know, Daddy. We're in the FBI office in Las Vegas and they're asking us a bunch of questions about Terry."

"I've been watching it on TV and it's all such a mess. Obviously they have the wrong guy. Terry wouldn't do anything like this."

Terry had always been one of my dad's favorite people. He trusted him completely, and had even blamed me when Terry and I got a divorce. Terry could do no wrong in my dad's eyes. After I left Michigan, they continued to be friends and had joined forces on some investments. At one point they had considered buying some property together in Arkansas and southwest Missouri.

"Don't you say anything that could hurt Terry," he warned, and for some reason I immediately thought about the FBI phones being tapped and worried that when they heard my dad say this they might think I would hold something back.

"I'm only answering the questions they ask me, Daddy. I really don't know anything." I felt like a little girl being lectured. "I'll call you again when I get home," I said, trying to ease off the phone.

Even if Terry was involved, my dad would never believe it.

Josh came plodding into the office as I was dialing my sister, Kelli, and plopped himself down in an armchair across from Alan Gough's desk. His big round face held no expression, but there was sadness in his eyes. I could tell he was as confused and as much at a loss as I was.

My sister was relieved to hear from me.

"I've been calling you," she said excitedly. "James has been arrested and Terry has turned himself in. What do you know, Lana? Where are you? I've called your house a hundred times."

"We're at the FBI headquarters in Las Vegas," I explained again. "We're okay, but I guess they think Terry and James had something to do with or know something about the bombing in Oklahoma. I certainly don't know anything about it."

Kelli was twenty-nine, and had once been married to James Nichols, Terry's brother. They had a nine-year-old son, Chase.

People always seemed intrigued to learn that two sisters had married two brothers; however, I'd usually quip, "It was a small town and there wasn't much to choose from," when they asked how it came to be. Truth was James had met Kelli one night when she had come over to baby-sit Josh at the Decker house, where Terry and I lived with James and my older boys.

James and I were never really close, although we tolerated each other during my marriage to Terry. James was more flamboyant and boisterous than Terry and enjoyed bossing Terry around. They'd had plenty of fights about it, some of them probably fueled by my urging Terry to be more aggressive and not take so much crap from James.

Kelli and I agreed to call each other as soon as we had more news, and hung up. I quickly dialed my office to check in with Kay, who had paged me at least a dozen times.

"I'm still here," I said, half kidding. "I think they're about finished, so we should be getting out of here soon. Any messages?"

There was a stack of them but none so urgent it couldn't wait until tomorrow.

Josh asked if he could use the phone to call his grandmother, and since Gough wasn't back yet, I said okay.

Joyce Nichols was a tough woman, and without question the driving force of the Nichols family. She had filed for divorce from Robert Nichols in 1974, after twenty-five years of marriage, and the split nearly crushed Terry, who was just a year out of Lapeer West High School.

Joyce had gotten a very generous settlement when the couple divided up their many properties and had kept the ranch house where they had lived. Terry's father had moved to one of the farms he'd acquired in the divorce, a sizable spread in Imlay City, Michigan, about twenty miles from the old place.

Despite the fact they had been separated for a year before divorcing, Joyce did not take the dissolution of her marriage gracefully. Robert Nichols recalls her driving into a field and ramming his tractor, destroying her car. On several other occasions she threatened her ex-husband with a gun.

According to the *Dallas Morning News*, Lapeer County law-enforcement officials remembered a number of instances when Joyce Nichols was drunk, rowdy, and physically as well as verbally abusive. Most notable of these was the time she tried to attack Patrolman Bill Dougherty with a chain saw. At the time she was a hit-and-run suspect trying to resist arrest.

Dougherty, who is now the Lapeer police chief, was

quoted as saying, "If she could have gotten that saw started, she would have done something bad with it." Charges against her were later reduced and she pleaded guilty to drunken driving.

Terry had shared with me his concerns about Joyce's drinking, but this didn't keep her from prospering at her own farm or from maintaining a stranglehold over her sons, who jumped whenever she raised her eyebrows.

It was late in the day back in Michigan, which usually meant Joyce would be pretty far "gone," but Josh dialed anyway. She had remarried and was now Joyce Wilt.

After exchanging hellos, there was a brief silence, then Josh blurted into the phone, "My dad didn't do this, Grandma. I know he didn't." The conversation lasted less than two minutes and I didn't speak to her. Joyce and I had never really been close, I guess because she objected so strongly to Terry marrying me, even threatening to disown him if he did.

She had told Terry I was "used goods," because I had two kids and had been married twice before. In her eyes I wasn't good enough for Terry. I wondered what she thought now.

Alan Gough returned and I asked if they were through and could we go home. He said he'd check with the director.

A minute later Randy Prillaman was sitting next to me, speaking in very deliberate tones. "I think, for your safety and the safety of your family, you should stay with us for a few days," he said. "Until we know more about this and until it dies down a little in the press. The media is not going to let you rest."

Then he dropped a bombshell.

"You know," he started slowly, "if this thing doesn't turn out well, you might even consider entering the Federal Witness Protection Program."

I wasn't hearing this. For a moment I was too stunned

to react. What the hell was he saying? Witness Protection!

"You mean like going undercover?" Josh asked.

"Sort of," Prillaman responded.

"But I'm a businesswoman, and I like it here in Las Vegas," I added, suddenly feeling very vulnerable. "I'm not going anywhere. We didn't do anything." I didn't want him to know I was frightened by what he was saying.

I had worked hard to build my business and it was just beginning to turn the corner. I wasn't giving it up because of a bombing in Oklahoma, no matter who did it. I mean, who would want to take revenge on us? Josh and I didn't do it. Why should we suffer?

"I didn't mean to alarm you, Mrs. Padilla." The director hadn't expected so vehement a response. "I just wanted to make you aware of some options. Certainly it is much too early to make any decisions like that. Let's just wait and see what develops."

We could have protested, but he was right. We didn't know what was out there. They were the FBI. They certainly had a lot better idea than we did if we were in danger or not. Trusting, we just went along with the program.

It was obvious they weren't sure if the bombing was a conspiracy, or how much danger my family and I were in, but what they did know for sure was that everyone connected with the FBI across the country was tense and on red alert. Any and all leads were to be pursued with vigor.

And most important for Gough, Prillaman, and the Las Vegas FBI, they were sitting on the case's hottest lead. The way things were shaping up, twelve-year-old Josh Nichols just might have been in the right place at the right time and could possibly be the closest thing to an eyewitness anyone had.

What a coup if they could break the ugliest crime of

terrorism in American history themselves, without any help from Washington. It would make other bureau offices from Quantico to New York, and some of their snide and pompous directors, stand up and take notice. No longer would Vegas FBI agents be referred to as desert rats, stuck in the neon capital of the world with nothing more important to do than baby-sit organized-crime types who wanted to launder money through casinos.

Despite his gentlemanly manner, Prillaman had to be salivating.

In his office he had two people who might be able to give him the answers to nail the bastards who blew up the Oklahoma City Federal Building, and they were being fully cooperative.

Even though some of the information was routine and valueless, we were spilling our guts, and unlike all of the hard-ass wiseguys he usually dealt with, we hadn't even thought to ask for a doggone lawyer. How sweet was that?

3

EACH TIME I MANAGED TO GET A SHORT BREAK
from Agent Gough's questions, I'd look in on the various offices where Josh, Barry, and Troy were being
interrogated. The discussions with Barry and Troy
were mundane and without much interest. They had
not had any actual contact with Terry in years other
than the few days he visited in November, so they
knew nothing of his habits or friends of the past five
years.

"We're about done," was the consensus of the agents
questioning each of them. "I think we've covered what we
needed."

When I slipped into Director Prillaman's office, where
Debbie Calhoun was still isolated with Josh, I got a different feeling.

Calhoun, a small, solidly built woman in her late thirties or early forties, smiled as I stepped in and closed the
door behind me. She had medium-length blond hair and a
round, cherubic face that belied her tenacity.

Like the other agents, she, too, was just wrapping up
when she tossed a soft curve at Josh in a Columbo-type
fashion. "By the way, Josh," she began, almost as an
afterthought, "I don't think I asked if you'd seen or ever
been around any type of explosives during the years you

lived on the farm in Decker or the time you spent in Herington on your vacation."

"Some," he said, almost whispering.

"What kind of stuff?" Debbie prodded.

"Different kinds of things," Josh answered hesitatingly. "My dad has a lot of guns. We shoot and we make some little bombs sometimes."

I was standing only a few feet away, only half listening, but the word "bomb" struck me like a gunshot.

Debbie didn't let on if she was surprised. It was a pivotal moment. Her next question could back Josh off or open him up. I waited to see how she would play it.

Josh saved her a decision.

"I know how to build a bomb," he said with the innocence of a kid bragging to his folks that he had learned to fly a kite or ride a bike.

I almost dropped my Diet Pepsi can, and for a second I couldn't make myself turn to look at him. Debbie, who seemed as tired as we were a moment before, perked up and leaned forward, her ears suddenly the size of Bugs Bunny's.

"You do," she said, trying to let Josh lead the way. "Bombs are pretty complicated, aren't they?" She sounded patronizing, even condescending, but Josh didn't seem to notice.

"Not really." Josh realized he had her complete attention and that what he was saying was important. What had Terry been teaching him? What else did he know? Who did he know?

Like most separated or divorced parents, I did not interrogate my son when he returned home after a visit to his father. I trusted Terry. And whenever Josh came home, I'd only ask if he had fun, and always hoped he had a good time.

I didn't want Terry grilling him about what we did when the situation was reversed. I assumed they always did father-son type things and I was grateful to Terry for spending time with him and doing the kinds of things mothers don't usually do with their sons.

Did you blow up anything? or Did your dad teach you how to make a bomb? were questions that would never have occurred to me.

Director Prillaman and Agent Charlie Oates came in, neither aware of the significance of Calhoun's breakthrough.

"Josh here was just telling me he knows how to build a bomb," Calhoun said in mock admiration. Josh warmed to the idea of being center stage and having a handful of adults rapt while he performed. In a childlike way I think he felt pretty special knowing he could do something none of the grown men around him knew how to do.

"It really isn't hard," he said, stone-faced. "My dad and I used to build them all the time. You need a little gasoline, some ammonium nitrate, and . . . "

My twelve-year-old son didn't know how to play baseball, but he could describe how to build a damn bomb. . . . What was wrong with this picture?

I stood with my mouth agape as I listened to him detail the bomb-making process. It didn't matter whether he was talking about the kind of bomb that could blow up a tree stump or a building. That he knew how at all stunned us all.

FBI Director Prillaman listened intently to the remainder of the conversation.

There was an awkward silence when Josh finished.

"I think we've about had enough for one day," Prillaman said, not letting on how interested he was in what he had just heard.

"A couple more thoughts and we can wrap this up for the night. I'll have some of my men take you home so you can pick up some things, and we'll get you all checked into a hotel," he said, looking at me. "That way you can get some rest. I'm sure you guys are all pretty pooped. I know I am."

It was nine o'clock, and through the window I could see it was almost dark outside. We were back on daylight saving time, so there were still a precious few remnants of light fighting to keep from being overcome by the darkness. I was mentally and physically exhausted. I ached all over. And so much for my plan to get back to the office, although I did call Kay at home to fill her in.

"I don't see what you have to do with this, or why they need you there so long," Kay groused. She was very protective of me, sort of like a mother hen, and we worked well together.

Kay was the financial backbone of Esquire Realty and we really did complement each other. I was a people person, and the out-front driving force of the company, while Kay preferred detail work and numbers more than personalities. She kept all the dollars and cents in line, managed the office, and dealt with all the day-to-day business stuff, which freed me to recruit agents, promote the company, and sell houses. We had a vision of having an office with a hundred agents and we were well on our way. In less than eighteen months we had nearly fifty, and were making some waves in the Las Vegas real-estate community.

I wasn't inclined, nor was I in a position, to tell her all that was going on, so I tried to defuse her worries. "I think we're done with the questioning," I said, not sure I was sounding convincing. "But they are going to put us in a hotel for the night so we can avoid dealing with the press."

"Where are they taking you? Be sure it's a nice hotel, and that you call to let me know where you are."

"I don't know yet where they're taking us," I said, realizing it hadn't been discussed. We'd just put ourselves in their hands, which I had no reason to think wasn't okay.

They were the government. Weren't they supposed to be the good guys?

"I'll call you as soon as we know something, Kay. And don't worry. Everything's going to be fine. We're all okay."

Except for the fact that they think Terry blew up a building in Oklahoma and Josh knows how to build a bomb. Other than those few minor details, things are just peachy.

Troy decided he would go to a friend's house to spend the night if it was okay with the FBI guys.

"I don't have a problem with that," Prillaman said nonchalantly. "Just be sure we have a number so we can reach you if we have to."

"Give them Eddie's number," I put in. I knew he would have been uncomfortable going back to my house because he and I had had a squabble the week before and he had moved out. I'd told him what I thought of his girlfriend, that she was too young and not good enough for him, and he took exception. He quietly finished drying the dishes, put the towel down, walked out of the kitchen into his bedroom, and packed his stuff.

There wasn't much else to say. I'd always been a straight shooter with my kids and I didn't think the girl was good for him. She was a high-school dropout and a street kid. She'd practically been abandoned by her mother and I told Troy in addition to sleeping with her, he'd better be prepared to educate and raise her.

Troy was twenty-one and very bright. He'd been an excellent student all through high school and a year of college, and managed honor-roll grades with very little studying. Unlike his older brother Barry, however, he was a little slow when it came to girls.

He asked for the money I'd been holding for him and I went into the bedroom and got it. He'd been saving to buy a car and I hated to see him take it, but we had come to a definite stalemate. I couldn't just stand by and see him make a big mistake without trying to help him. He put the money in his pocket, called a friend for a ride, and split. I guess the girl meant more to him than I thought. At least for the time being.

Right now we were all glad to be getting out of the FBI building, no matter where we were going.

Troy hugged me, shook hands with Barry, who was two years older, and looked Josh right in the eyes. They were about the same height. Despite the difference in their ages, the boys had always been close, and both Barry and Troy, while not necessarily the greatest role models for Josh, were very protective of him. I knew they all loved one another and that gave me a good feeling.

"Hang in there, Josh. Don't let them wear you down. Just answer their questions honestly and this thing will be over before you know it." Troy was perceptive and he understood that Josh was the person in whom the authorities were most interested. Oddly, after Terry and I were divorced, and I left Michigan for Nevada, Troy stayed behind to finish at Cass City High School. He and Josh lived with Terry and it worked out well for all of them.

The agent assigned to drive Troy to his friend's house waited while he said his good-byes. In a minute Troy turned and the two of them walked down the corridor and disappeared from view.

"Do I have a minute to freshen up before we leave?" I asked no one in particular.

"Sure, go ahead," Agent Gough replied. "It'll take a couple minutes for us to brief the agents on the new shift anyway."

The bathroom wasn't such a good idea.

As I stood in front of the little washbasin staring into the mirror, I began crying again. I put both hands on the sink to keep from falling. I felt weak and faint, like I was losing control and slipping into unconsciousness. I was scared.

I tried to steady myself and put on fresh lipstick, but couldn't keep my hand from shaking.

All right, Lana. Calm down. Take a few deep breaths. All of this will go away in a few days and things will get back to the way they were. Don't overreact. It's only a couple days out of your life.

Bolstered by my own pep talk, I regrouped, straightened my skirt, put on my "I'm not fazed by all of this, and even if I am I can handle it" face, and returned to the main conference room.

It's funny how, no matter who we are or how secure we are, we unravel when something traumatic invades our lives. On the surface, despite my occasional little crying bouts, I was handling things, but inside I was a wreck.

Being the oldest of eight children, I'd always been expected to handle whatever little slings life dished out, and I had, throughout my life. This time, though, it looked like I'd need a suit of armor.

The agents surveyed the FBI parking lot carefully before leading us to the waiting cars.

Josh, Barry, and I piled into a big brown Suburban driven by one Charlie Sanders. It was an improvement on Agent Gough's Plymouth Prillaman, Gough, and Debbie Calhoun stayed behind, presumably to transcribe notes and report whatever they thought important to Washington or whoever was in charge.

According to the television reports, Attorney General Janet Reno was going to supervise the investigation personally, and both she and President Clinton had announced at press conferences that the government would seek the death penalty against the person or persons convicted of bombing the Alfred P. Murrah Federal Building. Maybe they were going to call her. Was what we had to say that important? Probably not.

We had a whole new contingent of agents to escort us

home. I was disappointed that Gough had gone off shift. I felt comfortable with him. He made me feel as if we were people. Real people. As if we counted and weren't just pieces of evidence.

Three other cars, one in front and two behind, created a convoy to escort us home. We must have looked like a mini–political motorcade as we headed south on Eastern Avenue past the well-lit McCarran Airport runway to our home at 7160 Nordic Lights Drive.

It was a small, 1,300-square-foot, three-bedroom single-story tract home. Nothing fancy, but it was functional and it had a pool. I loved the water, even though I wasn't much of a swimmer, and so did Josh, and with the mild Las Vegas climate we'd worn out a couple of swimsuits in the year we'd owned the house.

Nothing was stirring in the neighborhood when we arrived, which was just as well because I didn't want the neighbors to see us getting out of the FBI cars in the company of federal agents. Up until now we'd been a pretty normal family with very little commotion around our house.

It felt good to be home, but none of us got to savor the feeling very long.

"Just pick up a few things," said Agent Sanders, who was clearly the senior man in charge. "Basics. Like toothpaste, underwear, a couple changes of clothes, socks . . . "

"How long will we be gone?" I asked, planning to protest if he said more than a day or two. Sunday was the limit. I absolutely had to be back at work on Monday. This nonsense had to be over by then. I'd go along till Sunday.

"I'm not sure exactly how long you'll be gone, Mrs. Padilla," the agent nearest me answered. "We'll just have to wait and see what happens tomorrow. Your safety is our primary concern." It sounded like a well-rehearsed statement.

We were all frantic, tossing socks, underwear, bras, and baseball cards into duffel bags.

The kids didn't notice that two of the five agents had remained outside. It wasn't necessary for them to be in the house, but I had a hunch they had other motives for not coming in. They were just standing, casually talking, in the manner of limo drivers waiting for their VIP clientele to return. Knowing they were out there should have made me feel safer; however, the realization that they were real-life bodyguards affected me in just the reverse way. For the first time I worried about our safety. If Prillaman thought he needed four cars and five agents to get us safely home and to a hotel, maybe we really were in danger. Was he just being cautious? Was I just being paranoid?

Who did he think was going to harm us? Certainly not Tim McVeigh or Terry. They were both in jail. Besides, Terry wouldn't do anything to us. We were his family.

Barry wanted to know if he should bring his guitar and Josh wondered aloud if he should pack his swim trunks.

"May as well," one of the agents replied. "I'm sure the hotel will have a pool."

We literally ransacked our own house, tossing clothes out of drawers and closets, stuffing anything we thought we might need in travel bags, and doing it at a furious pace.

In the backyard, I filled two dishes for the cat, changed the litter box, and made sure all the doors were locked. I had my pager in my purse, but I hadn't checked it since leaving the office in the morning. If I didn't answer by the third beep, it automatically went into my voice mail, so I knew I had a ton of messages. I'd check them from the hotel. Since I didn't have a recorder at home, I decided to forward my home phone to my pager. That way I wouldn't miss any messages.

All of us seemed to feel a sense of urgency about getting in and out, even though the agents never asked us to rush, and we were finished in less than twenty minutes. It was eerie.

"What hotel we going to?" Josh voiced the question I had wanted to ask.

"Circus-Circus. That okay with you?" Charlie Sanders was looking at Josh through the rearview mirror.

"Yeah. I guess." Josh was too tired to be excited by much of anything at the moment. "Can we order room service?"

"Anything you like." Sanders grinned. "It's on the FBI."

It was Friday night and the Las Vegas Strip was jammed. The combination of Vegas teens cruising and California weekenders gawking at the Mirage's erupting Volcano and the pirate sea battle at Treasure Island created bumper-to-bumper traffic that resembled the Santa Monica Freeway at rush hour. The lights were overwhelming, literally turning night into day, but we weren't there to sightsee.

We turned off the Strip as soon as it was feasible, cutting across Spring Mountain Road to Industrial Road. It was a straight run down Industrial to the back parking lot at Circus-Circus, and with only light traffic to contend with, we made it in less than ten minutes.

That was the good news.

The bad news was we had to wait in the car while three of the agents went in to get us registered and "secure" our rooms.

"Maybe they're bugging our rooms," Josh theorized.

"Could be," Barry agreed.

After half an hour of twiddling our thumbs and listening to songs with too much bass and lyrics I could not understand, I wasn't so sure Josh and Barry weren't right.

It was a long time to wait when the rooms had already

been arranged and guaranteed before we left FBI head-quarters. Didn't the government have any juice or did they really need time to "wire" our rooms?

Finally we got the okay and began climbing out of the Suburban, which had been parked in a no-parking zone since our arrival. It was a comfortable vehicle, but definitely not one I'd buy. At five-one, I was so short I nearly had to jump to get to the ground.

The agents grabbed our bags. Sanders had taken care of the registration, booking us under Director Prillaman's name to try to keep the press from finding us.

"Do you really think they'll be trying that hard to find us?"

"I wish I could say no," he answered, looking at the little square business-card-sized room keys in his hand. "I don't know which key goes to which room," he confessed. The electronic entry cards didn't have room numbers printed on them.

"Josh and Barry are in a room with two double beds. You're in an adjoining room with a king-size bed."

"We'll sort it out in a minute," I said politely. Vegas had become so sophisticated. Front-desk clerks had to check three computers before they'd give you a room key and sometimes they still weren't sure the room was ready.

In the old days it was easier. The maids would just go upstairs, change the sheets, sweep out the heartaches, and call down to give the all clear.

As far as we knew, the agents left. I don't think any of them remained in the hotel, but if they did we didn't see them.

I unpacked my bathroom stuff, changed into some shorts and an old T-shirt, and unlocked the connecting door to the boys' room. They had the TV on already and were propped up on pillows watching it.

The phone rang as I came into their room and we

looked at each other with uncertainty. It had to be someone from the FBI. No one else knew where we were. I answered.

"Hello . . ."

"Hello, is this Lana Padilla?" a female voice on the other end inquired.

I knew it wasn't the FBI.

"Who's calling?" I was shaken and trying to stall.

"This is Sandy from Channel Thirteen." I hung up and immediately dialed the number the FBI had given me in case of an emergency or something unexpected.

"I think you should tell Mr. Prillaman that the press has found us already," I told the agent on duty.

Within five minutes Randy Prillaman called back.

"I'm sorry," he apologized. "Just an enterprising reporter. I guess registering under my name wasn't such a good idea either. Let's hope it's an isolated incident," he said. "If anyone else calls, just say they have the wrong number. We'll see how it goes tonight and transfer you to a different hotel tomorrow if necessary."

It was late. I was tired and I suggested to the boys we all try to get some sleep even though I knew none of us would. I went back to my room and tried to turn off my brain. I awoke about 3:00 A.M. and could hear the TV in Barry and Josh's room. At home they often went to sleep with it on, so I didn't bother to go in and turn it off.

What I didn't learn until months later was that Barry had cracked under the pressure and relapsed into his druggie habits. It was both ironic and sad to have Josh tell me Barry rolled his drugs on the nightstand as they lay awake that first night, wondering what it was all about.

I was up early on Saturday and had already showered and finished my room-service breakfast by the time the phone rang. It was 9:00 A.M.

"Good morning, Lana. This is Agent Calhoun." By now I recognized her voice. "I hope you guys slept well."

I found it odd that she didn't ask about the phone call from the newsperson or if there had been any others. I wondered if she had been briefed, or did she know because they really had bugged our rooms? I was thinking too much again.

"It's a few minutes after nine now. I wanted to be sure that ten o'clock was a good time for me to come by and pick you and Josh up. We'll probably only need you down here for a short time today."

"Ten will be fine," I replied as a still-sleepy Josh wrinkled his brow and looked at me with a "do we have to?" expression.

"It won't be necessary for Barry to come," she added. "He can just hang out at the hotel if he wants to." Barry wasn't even up yet. Josh, who usually liked to sleep until noon or later on nonschool days had come rolling into my room a little after 7:00 A.M. It was he who had ordered room service for both of us.

The FBI office was alive, with at least half a dozen agents busy on the phones. We'd heard Attorney General Reno say on the news that the government was going to utilize every available agent and follow every lead to solve the case. I guess she wasn't kidding.

I was ushered into Director Prillaman's office while Josh and Agent Calhoun ambled off to a separate area.

It was evident from the very first question on Saturday that Prillaman and the local FBI had a lot more information than they'd had the day and night before.

They had more background on Terry, wanted to know more about our relationship and its breakup, why he joined the army, and anything I could tell them about Josh's visit and the exact time of his return to Las Vegas.

Did Terry take him to the airport? Did he leave from Kansas City or Wichita? What airline did he fly? Who paid for his ticket? Was anyone with Terry when he took

Josh to the airport? Yes, Marife and their little girl, Nicole, as far as I knew. No, no one else.

Yes, Terry called me from the Kansas City airport.

"Why Kansas City? Wasn't it farther from Herington?"

Yes, but the ticket was cheaper and I had paid for the ticket. I usually paid for the ticket when Josh went to visit Terry. I figured I could better afford it than Terry.

"Why? And what exactly did Terry do for a living?"

I had to admit I didn't know. Except for the gun shows.

"He does all kinds of things," I said, trying to make them understand that Terry always managed to find work to support his family.

"I know he does odd jobs. Farming sort of stuff. And he does gun shows with Tim. At least he did for a while. Terry told me he and Tim had some sort of falling-out a couple months ago and they wouldn't be doing any shows together anymore. He said he'd be doing it on his own. He buys and sells guns and other gear at shows all through the Midwest."

No, I didn't know the number of guns he had or how much they cost or how he got the money to buy them in the first place. Yes, he did have money from our division of property when we divorced.

Then the letters again. The damn letters.

No I didn't know what "CG 37" meant. Nor did I know what "Liquidate 40" meant. And I couldn't explain exactly why I thought he was going to commit suicide or "go undercover" when I first read the letters.

The "go undercover" was a sticking point.

Did I think Terry was a spy or a special agent of some kind? Did he ever say anything to give me that impression?

"Not that I can recall. No."

When did he meet Tim McVeigh? What were my impressions of McVeigh?

"I really don't know McVeigh very well" I said, "although I've spoken to him on the phone many times. He's always been polite and made conversation."

Did he seem moody or militant?

"Not to me. He was always cheerful."

What caused him and Terry to have a falling-out?

"I didn't know for sure. Terry only said that they were going to go their separate ways. He didn't say why. Maybe Josh knew. He knew Tim better than I did. Maybe his dad told him why."

Did I know who Ted Parker was, or why Terry needed an alias?

No. I didn't know who Ted Parker was and I didn't know Terry had ever used an alias. But neither did I know that at that very minute Josh was telling Debbie Calhoun that he had heard his dad use the name Ted Parker and that one of the reasons he didn't spend more time with his dad when Tim was around was because his dad told him Tim didn't like kids.

"Maybe I should go and check in on Josh," I said, and Director Prillaman agreed. I think he sensed my concern, and he wanted me to be assured that his agents were not browbeating a twelve-year-old.

Prillaman walked me down to the room where Debbie Calhoun and Josh were meeting, and I stepped in without disturbing them. Both looked up when I entered, but their conversation continued smoothly.

Was Tim ever mean to him? Josh said no. Had he seen Tim during his Easter visit to his dad? No, but Tim had called a bunch of times and on Sunday (April 16) Tim called demanding that Josh's dad come to Oklahoma City to pick him up because his car had broken down.

I had only been half listening to the quickened question-and-answer, my mind on a million other things. But when Josh started talking, his statements made me realize why the FBI, so desperate for any shred of evidence in this incredible case, hung on every word this important eye-witness uttered.

"Tim was talking so loud I could hear him from where I was sitting about ten feet away on the couch," Josh remembered. "I think the thing that finally convinced my dad to go was Tim telling him he had the television set my dad had asked him to pick up."

Debbie Calhoun continued to listen carefully. She had gotten Josh to trust her. To open up.

"My dad didn't have a TV in his house in Kansas, and just the day before Marife had been nagging at him to get one," Josh told her. "My dad had stored an old TV in my mom's garage in Las Vegas and had asked Tim to stop by and pick it up on his way to the Midwest. Tim lived in Kingman, which was just ninety miles from Vegas, so he agreed.

"My dad was still annoyed about Tim's call, and so was I. I only had one more day to spend in Kansas and I had hoped my dad and I could do something fun together. It would take him all day to drive to Oklahoma City and back.

"But Tim insisted it was urgent, and my dad said he had to go. He tried to cheer me up by telling me when he came back, we'd hook up the TV. I didn't care. I would rather have had my dad stay home.

"I even begged my dad to let me go with him, but he said it would be uncomfortable for the three of us in the truck. It was three hundred and forty-six miles from Herington to Oklahoma City. My dad left around one in the afternoon and came back just before two A.M."

Agent Calhoun was as still as a hunter awaiting his prey, making only critical notes in order that her scrib-bling not interrupt Josh's recollections.

"I had waited up for him and he was happy to see me.

"'What are you doing still up?' he asked me. He tried

to pretend he was upset, but I could see the grin on his face."

"Waiting for you," I said. "I just wanted to be sure you got home safe. Somebody's got to watch out for you."

It was as much of an apology as Josh would get for Terry being gone for so many hours.

When Josh told about his dad going to church, I was more than mildy surprised. Terry was an avowed atheist who had repeatedly told me he didn't believe in anything. After church, Terry, Marife, and Nicole went out to breakfast. Josh skipped church, deciding to sleep in.

On Monday, with the TV hooked up, Terry, who could never be accused of being frivolous, stuck to a promise he'd made to take Josh to the video store.

"I got *The Lion King, Tank,* and *Ace Ventura,*" Josh recalled for Calhoun. "I wanted to get another one, but my dad said three would be all I'd have time to watch before we had to leave for the airport."

Later, the FBI not only visited Catlin's IGA Grocery and Video in Herington to check the records, but also checked the running times of the three movies to be sure Josh had sufficient time to watch them in one afternoon.

"Marife and Nicole watched *The Lion King* with me," Josh remembered. "I think they only watched part of *Ace Ventura.* But when the last movie was over my dad said it was time to go, so I finished packing my stuff and we all crammed into his truck.

"It took about three hours to get to the Kansas City airport from Herington and we stopped for dinner at the Sirloin Stockade on the way. We still made it there in plenty of time to catch my eleven-twenty flight for Vegas.

The Saturday questioning went from 10:00 A.M. until around three in the afternoon, when one of the agents delivered us back to Circus-Circus. Barry was still in his room, watching TV and talking on the phone.

Josh wanted to go down to the carnival midway for recreation, and since the FBI had not put any restrictions on our movements, as long as we stayed in the hotel, I saw no harm.

"I want you to be back up here in an hour," I warned. "We're going to go to dinner at six-thirty."

"Barry, too?" Josh asked.

"All three of us."

After dinner, Barry said he wanted to go out for a while.

"I told a couple of my friends I'd meet them at Slots-A-Fun," he said, expecting an argument.

The FBI hadn't taken him for questioning that day, and seemed to be keeping him in custody just for his own protection, so I saw no harm in him going out with his friends.

"Call later to let us know you're okay," I said softly. "And try not to be too late."

Famous last words.

Barry didn't call until 7:30 Sunday morning.

"Mom? Just wanted to let you know I'm okay. I should be there in a little while."

I could tell he was high.

"Are you okay, Barry? Have you been doing drugs?"

He didn't answer, but he didn't have to. We didn't hear from him the rest of the day.

We did, however, hear from FBI Director Prillaman, who called to see how we were and to advise that someone would be there about 10:30 to pick us up.

By now we knew the drill. We'd be driven to the FBI building, where they'd go over new information with us. Many of the leads regarding Terry and Tim that had surfaced in various parts of the country over the past twenty-four hours would be filtered through us to see what we could corroborate or add to the mix.

We were beginning to feel like guinea pigs, but we

didn't know what else to do but cooperate. There was really no one we could turn to.

The Sunday session was relatively short, only three and a half hours. Were they running out of questions or were they as tired as we were?

When we returned to the hotel, there were no messages from Barry. Josh ordered room service and we ate while watching the news and crying. It was becoming a routine.

Tim McVeigh and Terry Lynn Nichols were the lead story on every channel.

Prillaman called back at eight o'clock to say he had arranged to move us to a different hotel on Monday.

"Whoa," I protested. "You said we'd be done by Monday and we could go home. I don't want to be cooped up anymore."

"I know you don't, Mrs. Padilla. We don't want to keep you any longer than we think is necessary. Right now I think it's necessary. There are a lot of kooks and crazies out there. Anyone who thinks your ex-husband did this terrible thing might want to take revenge on you or Josh. Our job is to prevent that from happening."

At least he didn't come out and say he believed Terry was responsible for the bombing.

The latest news reports all seemed to point the finger at McVeigh. They were claiming he had planted the bomb, and had rented a truck along with another man, who was being identified only as John Doe #2. The second man did not look like Terry, and for a moment I felt hope. Hope that maybe it was some bizarre mix-up.

"What about Josh going to school?"

"I don't think that's such a good idea right now," said Prillaman. "I'd suggest you think about keeping him out this week. With what's going on, I think he'd have a tough time concentrating."

Little did he know that Josh had been having a tough

time concentrating and following through for most of the semester. He wouldn't miss school a bit. I gave up protesting, knowing he was probably right about waiting until things died down.

The local press as well as the national press had bombarded my home and office with urgent messages. Since my home number was forwarded to my pager voice mail, I had to unload the messages every couple hours to be sure there was room for more messages.

Futilely, I tried calling Barry. Because the calls were being forwarded, I kept getting my own voice mail. If he was at the house, he couldn't answer when the phone rang. To him it probably seemed like he was getting lots of hang-up calls. He could call out but was unable to receive a call.

Late Sunday night Josh and I were propped up on pillows watching CNN. We had been spending so much time in our rooms we felt as if we were the prisoners.

The screen flashed a picture of Tim, in bright orange jail clothes, being escorted out of the courthouse in Oklahoma. He was handcuffed and shackled. His hair was in a crew cut and his face was blank.

Josh watched him intently, then got up from the bed, walked over, and clicked off the TV in silence. He then turned and looked at me, visibly distraught.

"Tim did it, Mom." He said it with an evenness in his voice that belied his twelve years.

"How do you know that, Josh?"

"I just do. Trust me."

4

IT WAS MONDAY MORNING. JOSH WASN'T IN SCHOOL, I wasn't at work, and the nation was mesmerized by the tragedy in Oklahoma City. Pictures of the pain and devastation were everywhere. And the body count kept rising.

In addition to being concerned about Terry, and what impact this situation was going to have on our lives, I was worried about Barry.

We hadn't heard from him since his call early Sunday morning when he had assured me he'd be back in the hotel "in a little while."

As far as the FBI was concerned, we had adjusted to the schedule. They'd pick us up at 10:30 A.M., take us to their offices, and ask questions based on information being funneled to them from various bureau field offices.

So far, Tim was the only one formally charged in the bombing. James and Terry were being held as material witnesses because of certain explosives found on James's farm and the large cache of weapons confiscated from Terry's house in Kansas.

But that was explainable because Terry bought and sold weapons at gun shows. He'd always had guns, even when we were married, and he was very meticulous about recording their serial numbers and descriptions.

Everything I'd read insisted McVeigh was maintaining

a strict silence, giving law-enforcement officials only his name, rank, and serial number and claiming he was a prisoner of war. Someone had also mentioned that Sunday, April 23, was McVeigh's twenty-seventh birthday. As if anyone cared.

Nothing I'd seen in print could convince me that Tim was very bright, which bothered me for an odd reason. Because even though I believed Terry was innocent, if the two of them were involved, Terry would have to have been the mastermind. Tim wasn't smart enough.

And when Agent Calhoun told us how Tim had been apprehended, I breathed a little easier. Terry couldn't have planned the bombing. He would have been so much more precise. He was a stickler for details and covered every possibility.

"Tim was originally stopped on Wednesday, at ten-thirty in the morning, sixty-three miles north of Oklahoma City, about an hour and a half after the bombing," Calhoun answered when Josh asked. "An Oklahoma state trooper pulled him over because his car didn't have current license-plate tags."

"I'm surprised Tim didn't just shoot him then," Josh said casually, but with authority in his voice .

"Why do you say that?" Agent Calhoun's interest was piqued.

"Because Tim always carried a gun." Josh said it as if he assumed that Agent Calhoun and the rest of the FBI should know.

"I believe he did have a gun," Calhoun speculated. She fished through a stack of papers trying to locate a copy of the arrest report.

"Here it is." Her hazel eyes scanned the paper quickly. "McVeigh did have a weapon. Apparently the trooper who arrested him, a man named Charlie Hanger, noticed a bulge inside McVeigh's jacket and took the weapon before Tim could use it."

"I knew something like that had to have happened," said Josh, satisfied that his theory about McVeigh had panned out.

Agent Calhoun didn't bother to mention that the 9mm Glock semiautomatic pistol Trooper Hanger confiscated from McVeigh's shoulder harness holster held a full clip of Black Talon "cop killer" bullets and that the trooper had held his own gun to McVeigh's temple in order to disarm him.

On the front seat of the 1977 Mercury Marquis, agents found correspondence vowing revenge against federal authorities for their part in the bloody confrontation and destruction of the Branch Davidians and their leader, David Koresh, in Waco.

The hell of it was that McVeigh had almost gotten away clean.

While all the world looked for the terrorist who had detonated the bomb, McVeigh sat silently for two full days in the Perry County jail, located on the fourth floor of the Noble County Courthouse Building. Then, on Friday morning, just minutes before he was due to go before the Noble County Court for a $500 bond hearing that would probably have seen him released and back on the street, he ran out of luck.

Noble County Assistant District Attorney Mark Gibson received an emergency call from the FBI advising that a prisoner being held in the Perry jail, one Timothy James McVeigh, was not, under any circumstances, to be released. He was the prime suspect in the bombing of the Alfred P. Murrah Federal Building.

Gibson rushed a note to District Attorney John Maddox and McVeigh was detained. Word spread through the small town like an infectious disease. In minutes the entire population knew the suspected bomber was being held in their jail and an angry crowd quickly formed outside the courthouse. Half an hour later a brace of army helicopters descended noisily on the once unknown town of Perry, landing just outside the town square.

Now, instead of gaining his freedom, the former army demolitions expert was kept in custody, and by nightfall America was seeing footage of an orange-clad McVeigh, handcuffed and shackled, being led down the steps of the courthouse in Perry.

Inexplicably McVeigh was not wearing a bulletproof vest as he walked through the crowd, and the first thing to cross my mind was John F. Kennedy and his accused assassin, Lee Harvey Oswald. Marching McVeigh through a hostile crowd, charged with emotion from the bombing, was a careless and risky thing to do.

I wondered if the FBI wanted McVeigh to end up with the same fate as Oswald. It certainly would have been easier. No expensive trial. No waiting. Step right up for instant justice. Oklahoma style.

Amid cries of "baby killer," the crew-cut McVeigh, under heavy FBI guard, was transported by helicopter to Tinker Air Force Base, where he was charged with maliciously damaging federal property.

I had picked up every paper available on Sunday and spent the entire day trying to piece together clues from the incredibly diverse reports. I knew from the questioning that many of the articles contained inaccuracies and speculation. Some of them, however, reported facts that had to have been leaked. That was the only way reporters could have gotten the information, because the FBI kept telling us certain things were "confidential," and the next day or so those same sensitive items would appear in print, attributed to "a source close to the investigation" or "a well-placed government official." Never any names, just vague attributions.

I soon learned that different FBI sources frequently "leaked" department ideas to favored reporters to get public reaction or in the hope that it would elicit some response from the suspects. It was my first experience with the mind games that were to become a big part of the case for us.

That was certainly true of the John Doe #2 theories. At first, we were told John Doe #2 might be a Middle Eastern type, but this rumor quickly evaporated. The Bureau circulated a composite sketch of a dark-complected, square-jawed man in his late twenties or early thirties with a tattoo on his left arm, along with a small incentive for anyone turning him in—a $2 million reward!

It was supposed to be a drawing of the man who had been with McVeigh when he rented a Ryder truck from Elliott's Body Shop in Junction City, Kansas. The truck was rented on Monday, April 17, the same day Josh came home.

The manhunt for John Doe #2 was the most exhaustive in United States history. No matter what line of questioning the agents pursued on any given day, they always came back to the mystery accomplice. For some reason, they believed Josh could identify him.

That was a logical deduction. Josh knew all of his dad's friends, knew McVeigh, and was close at hand during the time frame when the truck was rented. Agent Calhoun was positive Josh had been present when the truck was rented, and wouldn't back off from this conviction.

And through it all, whenever a lead showed the slightest possibility that it might connect to a legitimate suspect, they would beat a path to Josh to see if he could identify the picture. Terry had already been ruled out as John Doe #2, and they thought Josh could positively identify McVeigh's accomplice.

A clerk at the Ryder office had identified McVeigh, who used a phony license with the name Bob Kling and a bogus South Dakota address on the rental application, but could provide only a vague description of his companion. McVeigh had lied and said he was going to drive the truck to Omaha.

"That's what he told my dad to say, too," Josh blurted.

Debbie Calhoun looked at him quizzically.

"When Tim called on Sunday asking for my dad to come and pick him up, he told my dad to tell Marife he was going to Omaha, not Oklahoma City. That's what my dad told her, but he told me the truth."

Agent Calhoun did not miss the message that Terry trusted Josh more than he trusted his wife, and that he didn't try to hide things from his son.

She immediately began to try to home in on a timetable to clarify the type of details that could help establish the extent of Terry's involvement, if any. Calhoun was the local specialist in dealing with children, and at this point, as if she sensed a chance to cover some unmarked ground, her demeanor became slightly more predatory.

Josh shifted in the chair as she resumed the questioning, and I thought it better to leave them alone. That way Josh could speak freely in case he had something to say he didn't want me to hear.

As Josh told me later, the questions came at him with the rush of a sudden hailstorm.

"How often did Tim call your dad during the week you were there?"

"I'm not sure . . . maybe once a day, sometimes twice."

"Was there a Ryder truck parked behind your dad's house at any point during the time you were there on vacation?"

"No. I never saw one."

"Could it have been there and you didn't see it?"

"No. My friends and I played back there like all the time."

"Have you have ever heard of the Dreamland Motel?"

"Yes."

"Did you ever go there or stay there?"

A slight hesitation, then: "No. I've never been there."

"But you do know where it is."

"Yes. In Junction City, Kansas."

"Did you know Tim McVeigh stayed there?"

"Yes."

The answer surprised Agent Calhoun and she jumped on it.

"How did you know Tim McVeigh was there? Did your dad visit him there? Did you go with your dad to visit McVeigh at the Dreamland? Did your dad say anything about going with Tim to rent a Ryder truck?"

It was a little fast for Josh. He didn't know which question to answer first. His voice got a little frosty.

"I told you I've never been to the Dreamland. . . ."

"Then how do you know about it?"

"Because my dad told me Tim was staying there."

And before Agent Calhoun could ask for details: "One day after he had just hung up with Tim, I asked if Tim was in town or coming over. He said no, Tim was in Junction City at the Dreamland, and he wouldn't be able to make it by this trip because he had business to take care of."

Meanwhile, in another office, Agent Gough was giving me the third degree, only in a less staccato fashion.

Was Terry a member of any paramilitary or militia group? Did I know if he ever attended any meetings of the Michigan Militia or anything like it?

No, I'd never heard of him going to any meetings.

Did he subscribe to any right-wing magazines or newsletters? Did he ever try to convince me that the government was corrupt? Did he ever try to get me to watch any political tapes? Was he angry about Waco? Did he complain about the government and bureaucracy in general? Did he like paying taxes?

Tell me somebody who *likes* paying taxes, I challenged. Did he complain about the government? No more than other people. He subscribed to *Soldier of Fortune* magazine, but he didn't really talk to me about it.

Was he angry about Waco and the Branch Davidian massacre? I think most Americans were angry and upset about the way it was handled. Terry had mentioned it, but he didn't dwell upon it.

Would it surprise me to know that a neighbor had spotted the Ryder truck used in the bombing parked behind Terry's residence at 109 South Second Street in Herington on April 17?

"At this point nothing would surprise me, Agent Gough. I'm so numb that if you told me Tim and Terry killed President Kennedy, I might believe it."

And I meant it. Every day, every hour, there was so much talk about Oklahoma and so many conflicting stories, who could know what to believe? One minute it appeared the evidence was overwhelming and the next it all seemed circumstantial and explainable. Disneyland had no roller coasters to match the one my emotions were riding.

Did my ex-husband murder a hundred or more innocent people or was he a pawn in a conspiracy plot?

Tim McVeigh was in a federal prison in El Reno, twenty miles west of Oklahoma City. Herington police had turned Terry over to the FBI and he was being held in a Wichita jail. Neither of them could leave. Josh and I were being held in Las Vegas. We could leave, but we always had to come back.

Terry had apparently made some statements to the FBI in Wichita, and from time to time, select portions of those statements were relayed to us during questioning.

In an effort to make me feel less of a traitor for talking about a man I'd been married to for eight years, Agent Gough showed me a statement that claimed one of

Terry's relatives described Terry as a friend of McVeigh's, and said they once lived together with James on the farm in Decker. The relative further stated that James Nichols and his brother, Terry Lynn Nichols were former members of the Michigan Militia, a right-wing organization that had engaged in extensive military training.

I wondered which relative was cooperating. The FBI wouldn't say.

It was now almost 5:30 on Monday, five days after the bombing and Terry's fourth day in FBI custody. Another day had passed and I could see that the questioning was not going to be over soon. There was no light at the end of the tunnel. I was prepared for Gough or Director Prillaman to approach me with some plausible story explaining why it would be necessary for them to keep us another night.

Ten minutes later my foreboding became a reality.

Phillaman had a "I know you know what's coming" look on his face as he sat down beside me. "I know you're really anxious to get back to your own house, Lana, and we'd like you to be there, but I would be remiss in my job if we had you return home while tensions are so high.

"The thing is, a lot of people were hurt or killed in Oklahoma City. It's possible some of them may have relatives here in Las Vegas, and in some twisted idea of revenge, they may come after you." Since I'd read stories about the anger of the people in Oklahoma and how many lives the bombing had touched, Prillaman's argument made sense.

He could have added, *Besides, we're not through with you. We had no idea you could add as much as you have to our investigation. We're all getting brownie points for the info you're providing. Who better to tell us about Terry and help us build a case than the people who lived with him.*

"Also, there have been a couple calls to your room at Circus-Circus which concern me a little bit. For that reason I'd like to move you and Josh to another hotel. I believe the agents are ready to take you back now, so if you'll just pack your things and get ready, they'll take you to the Excalibur and get you situated."

Josh liked the idea of transferring to the Excalibur, one of the newest mega-hotels on the strip, with more than 3,300 midpriced rooms. He also enthusiastically embraced the idea of being out of school another day or so. The hotel was designed like a huge medieval castle and was one of the most popular of Las Vegas's new wave of theme hotels. While other Strip hotels fought over the constantly dwindling list of Vegas headliners, the Excalibur featured a nightly jousting tournament complete with white knights rescuing damsels in distress on a huge, dirt-floored riding arena. The hotel even carried the period theme through to its dinner show, offering cheering audiences an entree of Cornish game hen, broth, potato, and vegetable to be eaten peasant style, sans utensils.

The hotel was owned by the same company that owned Circus-Circus, had a midway, lots of arcade games and rides, and scores of strolling hotel personnel decked out in bright, satiny uniforms. It was a fun place. I only wished our mood could have been lighter so we could have enjoyed our stay.

I called Kay from my new room, but forgot to tell her the FBI had registered me under the alias of Denise Graham. Now I was a woman checked into a hotel under an assumed name. What next?

"The office just isn't the same without you," Kay said nicely. "We miss you. And, in case you didn't know, the media is still bombarding us with phone calls and letters. Even some faxes. Television news crews cruise by the office every day just in case you happen to stop by. They keep asking if you've gone into the government's Witness Protection Plan.

"You haven't, have you?"

"No, Kay, we haven't and I don't plan on it. This is taking a little longer than we expected, but it will all be over soon. I think they just want to be sure everyone out there understands Josh and I are completely in the dark about this whole thing.

"You know, we're victims just like those people in Oklahoma." It was the first time I had thought of us as victims, but the term fit. We had done nothing and were suffering. Maybe not physically, but mentally. And our lives had been turned upside down through no fault of our own.

"How much longer do you think you'll be gone?" Kay asked, and I could feel she was insecure about our future. The company needed me. And I needed to work. My being there was the only way both Kay and I could survive.

"I hope we can be home tomorrow night," I said wishfully. "They'll bring us in for more questioning tomorrow morning, then maybe let us go home in the evening."

"Well, they've had you since Friday," Kay huffed. "Tomorrow's Tuesday. That should be long enough.

"By the way, you've had a couple of calls from Diane Sawyer's office. From her assistant, Jamie Zahn. I was thinking, maybe you ought to talk to her. Tell her your story."

"Maybe I will talk to her," I said, mainly to pacify Kay. Then I got braver. "Listen, Kay, if we're not out of here by tomorrow night, I'll call her back on Wednesday, just to see what she has to say. Hold on to her number."

"I have it written in my book," she said to reassure me. "Is everything else okay? I mean under the circumstances."

"As well as can be expected," I lied.

On top of all my other worries, I had an underlying

problem—Barry. I hadn't heard from him since Sunday morning or seen him since Saturday night, and now that we'd changed hotels, there was no way for him to contact us. Even worse, I still couldn't call him because of the house phone having been call-forwarded.

I knew he wouldn't contact the FBI offices because he was probably strung out, and for that same reason I didn't want to alert them to the fact that I didn't know where he was. I was afraid they'd arrest him. I'd just have to wait it out and pray he was all right.

Agents Gough and Calhoun were cheerful and upbeat on Tuesday morning, and both were patient and helpful when Josh posed some questions of his own. I suppose he figured he'd answered enough to earn the right to ask some.

McVeigh, who in the beginning had officially been listed as John Doe #1, had now been positively identified by a second source, Lea McGown, owner of the Dreamland Motel. She confirmed that McVeigh had checked in on April 14 and checked out on April 18, the day before the bombing.

"What was the most important clue you've gotten so far?" Josh's question was so basic I wondered if he realized the enormity of the case. But how could he? He was only twelve years old. Even at forty-five, I couldn't grasp how deeply enmeshed we were in the unfolding nightmares. We were on the inside and right now we were too involved to be scared.

"One of our agents found a piece of truck axle two blocks away," Gough explained patiently. "It was just a twisted scrap of metal that had been blown that far from the force of the explosion. "The axle had a VIN number. Do you know what a VIN number is, Josh?"

"Yeah. A vehicle identification number."

"I'm impressed," I said truthfully.

"Me, too," said Agent Calhoun.

Gough explained that the agent fed the truck's VIN number into the Rapid Start System computer, which traced it to a 1993 Ford truck belonging to a Ryder rental franchise in Miami. The truck had been assigned to a rental company known as Elliott's Body Shop in Junction City, Kansas, 270 miles from Oklahoma City.

"Once we figured out where the truck came from, we sent a bunch of agents to Junction City to canvass the area," said Gough. "Unfortunately the licenses and ID provided by the men who had rented the truck turned out to be phony.

"But the Ryder rental agent was able to provide enough of a description for an FBI artist to put together some sketches."

"So that's how you got the drawing of Tim. Right?"

"Right. Then our agents walked all over Junction City, showing the drawings to bartenders, store owners, and people at motels. They got lucky when they got to the Dreamland, which you know is a half mile outside the town. The lady recognized the sketch of John Doe number one, remembered him being clean-cut and reclusive looking, and said he told her his name was Tim McVeigh.

"The agents fed McVeigh's name into our database, which is a national computer network we use to track suspects, and the computer located the recent arrest record of Tim McVeigh on a traffic-and-weapons charge in Perry, Oklahoma. We were doggone lucky he was still in jail."

"Pretty lucky," Josh agreed.

"Why do you think your dad hung out with someone like Tim McVeigh?" Debbie Calhoun asked, officially ending the informational interlude and putting the ball back in her court.

Josh was not fooled by her seemingly innocent phrasing. He recognized that she was trying to categorize Terry and Tim as two peas in a pod.

"I don't know," he replied.

"How do you think your dad got mixed up in all of this?" Calhoun asked. She was making a presumptive leap. I thought for a moment Josh might call her on it. I watched him carefully as he filtered the question through his brain.

"I guess my dad just picked the wrong friend," he said bluntly. He couldn't have given a better answer.

On Tuesday, Director Prillaman informed me that word had come down that the U.S. attorney's office in Oklahoma City was preparing a subpoena ordering me to appear before a grand jury.

"I haven't seen it yet, but I wanted you to know it was coming," he said, trying to downplay the significance of the document. "They'll probably send it to my office. The official subpoena probably won't get here for a few days. I'll let you know as soon as we get it."

"What exactly does it mean to get subpoenaed?" I asked. "And why would they have to subpoena me when I'm already cooperating?"

"The subpoena is just a formality," he explained. "It officially requests you to appear in Oklahoma City before the jury hearing the case. That jury is listening to all the evidence presented to try and determine if there is enough reason to charge Terry Nichols.

"It also means the government will pay for your transportation and lodging."

"And it means I have no choice about going, isn't that right?" I asked.

"I'm afraid so," he said in a very low voice. "If you refused to go, you could be held in contempt. But you'll be okay. They'll probably only go over some of the things you've told us. Sometimes they simply like to hear those things for themselves."

To him the subpoena was inconsequential. To me it sounded ominous.

There was no longer any point asking when we would get to go home.

Inside, I was still agonizing over Barry. I wouldn't for the life of me have admitted to anyone that each day I checked the *Las Vegas Review-Journal* obituary column hoping I wouldn't find his name.

I didn't even want to tell Kay about him. I would have been too embarrassed for her to find him all doped up, if in fact that was the condition he was in. Maybe he had just decided to lie low at a friend's house. It would have been okay for Kay to know that, but I didn't want to take the chance.

On Wednesday, after a short day of questioning, we returned to the Excalibur, with its majestic white towers and multicolored rooftops. Josh wanted to head for the arcade, and he did, raiding my purse for quarters. I had none, so he palmed a ten-dollar bill and bounded off.

I called Kay. It was 4:15 in the afternoon and she was the only one left in the office.

"Looks like we're going to be here at least one more day," I said glumly. "Do you still have Diane Sawyer's number?"

I knew she did.

"Right here. It's her home number. Do you want it?"

"No. I want you to dial it and connect us on three-way." If the FBI had the room phone tapped, they probably weren't too pleased with what they were hearing.

It was 7:30 in New York, and I fantasized about Diane Sawyer at home cooking dinner, then dismissed the thought as completely ludicrous. Sawyer intrigued me because she was a woman who had made it in a man's world. And made it to the top. Someone told me she made $7 million a year, which, if they were even close, meant she was not only good and tough, but wouldn't be cooking her own dinner.

She turned out to be as smooth and charming as she was on TV.

"First of all, thank you for returning my call," she said politely. "I am so sorry for what you're going through. This must all be so trying for you and your son. I can't imagine what it must be like."

She sounded genuinely concerned and it touched me. This important television person cared and understood.

"Thank you," I said, not wanting to sound awestruck. "It has been a very rough time, but Josh and I have made it through. We've been cooperating with the FBI and telling them everything we know. We don't know what else to do. We feel so badly for the people of Oklahoma."

I guess it was the hook she was hoping for.

"So many people were devastated by what happened," she said in a barely audible voice. "Maybe it would be good if you did an interview to tell the people of Oklahoma how sorry you are about what happened. Just whatever you feel."

"I really don't know if I'm ready for something like that."

"I'm going to be coming through Las Vegas on Friday night," she continued. "If you're finished with the FBI by then, why don't we just have dinner? We'll talk more about it then. No cameras, no pressure, just talk. Then, if you decide you want to do an interview, we can arrange to do it on Saturday."

I agreed. And she said I wouldn't have to do the interview if I didn't want to.

"I'll arrange for my assistant, Jamie Zahn, to fly into Vegas tomorrow. That way, if we can get together, she'll be prepared to take care of the details. It was nice talking to you, Lana, and I look forward to meeting you. I think your story is very important."

Thursday was another short day, with the focus falling on the elusive John Doe #2 again.

We were told that more than 40,000 calls regarding the mystery man had been handled at the FBI's 800 number, and they still had no solid leads. A newspaper article claimed the bombing had generated 60 percent more TV exposure than the remainder of the top-ten stories combined between April 17 and 28. I was astonished to discover that the bombing had gotten eight times as much coverage as the O. J. Simpson trial.

But why couldn't anyone find John Doe #2? Was he that clever? Had he left the country? Was he in hiding?

"Nothing, not the search for John Dillinger, James Earl Ray, the bombers of Pan Am Flight 103, or the dragnet for Patty Hearst compared to the exhaustive manhunt for John Doe #2," said crime scholar Jay Robert Nash, author of the *Encyclopedia of Crime.* "The forces aligned against him are absolutely enormous, more so than ever before in history."

There was a bail hearing for Terry in Wichita, Kansas, on Thursday and it provided answers to some lingering questions.

Terry admitted driving to Oklahoma City to pick up McVeigh on April 16, just as Josh had confirmed. He dropped McVeigh off in Junction City, at 1:30 A.M. and was back in Herington at 2:15 A.M.

During the drive, Terry said McVeigh told him, "Something big is going to happen."

Terry asked, "What are you going to do, rob a bank?"

McVeigh supposedly repeated his first sentence. "Something big is going to happen."

According to the affidavit, there was no further conversation to clarify McVeigh's statement.

Also contained in the affidavit was a complete list of the weapons and matériel taken from Terry's Herington, Kansas, house, a home I indirectly helped him purchase by vouching for his credit with the previous owner, who carried paper on the loan.

I was dumbstruck to learn that one of the weapons seized at Terry's farm was an antitank rocket. Other items included nonelectric detonators, four fifty-five-gallon plastic drums, books and brochures dealing with Waco, and a thick stack of antitax and antigovernment literature.

Terry had waived his Miranda rights when he turned himself in, referring to the process as "interrogation," and said that the latter "was a word which reminded him of Nazi Germany."

I didn't know what to tell Josh. I knew even less what I should tell myself. It felt like we had been away from home for a year, even though it hadn't been a full week.

"We're going to take you home this afternoon," Director Prillaman said shortly after Josh and I had eaten lunch. The department was pretty used to our lunch requests after six days. Wendy's, McDonald's, or Taco Bell. Coke and strawberry milkshakes for Josh, Diet Pepsi for me. We weren't hard to please.

"I want to thank both you and Josh for your cooperation and help," Prillaman said genuinely. "However, even though we're sending you back home, I want you to understand that we'll probably still require your cooperation as things develop.

"And, for your protection, I'm going to assign special agents to keep an eye on you."

Going home was both a relief and a nightmare.

The house was in a shambles. We opened the door to blaring rock music and a distraught Barry, who was so happy to see us he couldn't speak. His eyes were red, his face unshaven, and his long, almost shoulder-length brown hair, which looked like Andre Agassi's before the tennis pro had it shaved because it was thinning on top, was messy and unkempt.

"I thought I was never going to see you again," he babbled. "I kept trying to call you but couldn't get through.

Then the people on TV said you and Josh had gone into the Witness Protection Program. I didn't know what to do. I didn't want to go outside because the press has been camped out on the lawn and all over the street for the past three days. When I tried to go out, they followed me, shoving microphones in my face and asking me questions. I ran back in and have been inside ever since.

"And something's wrong with the phone. It only rings once then cuts off."

"It's been on call forwarding," Josh told him. "You could make calls out, but you couldn't get any in."

"I was going to sell my guitar to get some money to start looking for you," Barry said, tears streaming down his cheeks.

In his frustration he had kicked a hole in the wall and seemingly tossed everything in the house from one place to another. It wasn't a pretty sight.

A few minutes later Barry, Josh, and I were huddled together on the sofa, our arms tightly entwined. We were together. We were family.

5

WE WERE HOME AT LAST, BUT THINGS HAD changed forever. For sure we weren't the same people who had lived here a week ago.

I still couldn't believe the bombing had happened only eight days before.

It was Thursday, April 27. We had been gone six days. Long enough for my recently acquired orange tabby, Kitty, to disappear. She probably thought we had deserted her or, worse yet, because she hadn't been fed.

Our phone was listed and it rang every few seconds with reporters from practically every publication in the country hungry for information. Everyone wanted a personal interview either with accused bomber Terry Nichol's ex-wife or the son who had spent an entire week with his dad prior to the bombing.

Since I had rarely dealt with the media, it was all new to me. I was trying to be accommodating. I'd answer their questions as best I could, and in as much depth as I could. But it was never enough. There was always one more question, one more thing they wanted to clarify or didn't understand. And regrettably, I wasn't selective. I'd talk to whoever called. I wasn't sure if I was just flattered by all the attention or if it was my natural willingness to try to be helpful. Sunup to sundown I was a talking machine.

But it was give-and-take. I answered their questions, but I also gathered lots of information, and listening to what reporters in different areas of the country were going after, I formed theories of my own.

There had been dozens of messages and faxes sent to the office, business cards shoved in our screen door, and offers from a slew of television shows to fly Josh and me to their studios in New York, Atlanta, or Los Angeles.

NBC, CBS, ABC, *Geraldo, Larry King Live, The Today Show*, CNN, *Good Morning America*, the *National Enquirer, Star, Globe, Inside Edition, Hard Copy, American Journal*, the *Washington Post, New York Times, Las Vegas Sun*, and the *Las Vegas Review-Journal* all attempted to contact me.

Andy Warhol had passed away, but his philosophy was alive and well. Ready or not, this was my fifteen minutes.

I had phoned Kay from the FBI offices as soon as I was told we'd be going home, and she in turn called Diane Sawyer's assistant in Los Angeles.

Ms. Zahn had already flown from New York to L.A. in order to be closer to Las Vegas if the interview came together. When Kay called, Jamie booked a flight from LAX to McCarran and was arriving at nine o'clock that night. Kay had arranged to pick her up.

While we were unpacking and getting reacquainted with our house, Kay was meeting Zahn and transporting her to the Alexis Park, perhaps the most elegant non-gaming hotel in the city.

Kay called after she had finished playing taxi. "They've made arrangements for Diane Sawyer to come in tomorrow around noon," she reported. "The plan is for you to have dinner with her in the evening and decide at that time if you want to go through with an interview."

"What's Jamie Zahn like?" I asked, not really caring.

"Eager. Young. A little pushy. New Yorkish. She's okay."

FRIDAY, APRIL 28,1995

East Coast reporters began calling as early as 6:30 A.M., and when I looked out the kitchen window, I could see a television news truck parked across the street. A reporter with a microphone stood next to a cameraman. They apeared to be chatting aimlessly, but were on the alert in case something stirred at our house. I wondered if they had nothing better to do.

Sawyer called a little after one o'clock, inviting me to dinner at five o'clock at the hotel. She thought it might be nice if we had a quiet meal in her suite, away from the general public, and I concurred.

Headlines in the local papers screamed about the rising Oklahoma death toll. It had reached one hundred and more bodies were expected; however, rain was slowing rescue efforts. Many of the victims had been children in the building's day-care center.

The Alexis Park is only about fifteen minutes from my house, but I don't remember driving there. I was somber and withdrawn. Why was I doing this? I kept asking myself.

I picked up the house phone and asked for Ms. Sawyer's room. Was she Ms. or Mrs.? I didn't know, and it made me realize I didn't know anything about her except that she was on TV every week.

She answered cheerily on the second ring, gave me her room number, and I headed for the elevator.

Most of the dinner conversation was about Josh, and what we'd been through.

"I think people should see the pain you're in, let them feel it, too. Josh is just a boy. You're real people, and if you make a statement to the country, they will identify with you."

I wasn't thinking straight or I would have asked why. Why did we need to make a statement? We had nothing to do with what had happened.

I think Sawyer sensed she had me and it was just a matter of reeling me in. I was in over my head. Convincing people to go on camera and talk about things they really didn't want to talk about was her job. And she was good at it. She was, in a sense, the ultimate snake-oil salesman, offering me something I didn't need and making me believe I was lucky to get it.

"We can do it tomorrow, maybe around eleven or so," she said gently. "I'll have Jamie arrange a crew.

"And you know what, Lana? You'll feel good about this when it's over. Good about getting whatever you want to off your chest."

"But what if I change my mind later?" I wanted to know. "What if I decide I don't want to be on national television, or I say something I shouldn't?"

She could have answered anything and I would have bought it.

"If you change your mind, or you're not comfortable with the interview, for any reason whatsoever, all you have to do is call me and I'll pull it. You have my word on that.

"And I won't put you on the spot. I won't ask you or Josh any questions about Terry's innocence or guilt. This is more your statement. You can say whatever you choose."

I left with ambivalent feelings. On the one hand, I felt relieved. On the other, I was anxious. I had never done a TV interview and I wasn't sure I was doing the right thing.

SATURDAY, APRIL 29, 1995

We did the filming in one of the conference rooms at the Kay's members-only Canyon Gate Country Club. The cameras didn't seem to bother the well-bred regulars, many of whom seemed so engrossed in themselves and so aloof that I got the feeling they were pretending we weren't even there.

For her part, Diane Sawyer started out like a lamb, tossing some fluffy, easy-to-answer questions that helped me relax. Then she got more aggressive, homing in on Terry and our relationship, what type person he was, and Josh's visit before the bombing.

"Would it surprise you to learn there is a dark side to Terry?" she asked in that low whisper, as if she wanted me to share the answer with her alone.

Then: "Do you think he's capable of something like this?"

"No, I don't," I replied without hesitation. "But when I heard Josh tell the FBI that he knew how to build a bomb, I was shocked." That opened the floodgates. I had blurted it out without thinking and she all but licked her chops. After that, she went after the salacious details, occasionally mixing in some nonthreatening soft stuff, but the tone had changed.

It wasn't as much a chance for me to make a statement as it was a chance for her to score a news exclusive. She never asked me or Josh if we thought Terry was involved, but she played me like a banjo. I opened up and held nothing in reserve and she pounced on anything remotely sensational.

She asked Josh directly if he knew how to make a bomb, and when he said he did they had all the sound bite and promo material they'd ever need. She repeatedly came back to questions about the mystery package and Terry's letter to McVeigh, and dramatized the tragedy of the bombing. The story was a coup for Sawyer and *PrimeTime Live*. It was strictly business.

The interview took nearly four hours, and when it was over Sawyer thanked Josh and me profusely, told me again how much she empathized with us, and walked off to her waiting limo. She slipped easily through the door being held open by the chauffeur, slid lightly across the red leather seat, and opened a magazine.

I watched for a moment as the white stretch pulled away. She never looked back.

It's just another story to her, I thought. We were never really important. Who was I kidding? The "you have my number and I want you to call me if you ever need to talk" speech was just hot air. She probably says it to everyone she interviews.

But she had gotten what she came after. That's why they paid her the big bucks. *PrimeTime* hadn't paid a dime for the hottest story in the country. When I watched her drive off, I felt as cheated as a mistress watching her married lover get dressed to go home in the middle of the night.

The first three weeks of May were so hectic I came close to a nervous breakdown. I now look back and wonder how we survived.

Something eventful and earthshaking seemed to happen every day. Every hour. And much of it affected not only us, but all of America. We just happened to be living it in a more immediate way.

MONDAY, MAY 1, 1995

The reservations I had felt when Diane Sawyer departed on Saturday intensified over the weekend, and by Monday I had done an about-face. I wanted to take her up on her promise to allow me to cancel or pull the segment.

I felt exploited and misled and realized when we did the interview I must have still been in shock and not thinking straight. I also thought many of the questions were improper and could cast Josh in a bad light. Especially the references to bombs. I didn't want people to come away thinking he was going to grow up to be some sort of mad bomber.

Moreover, I was disappointed I had allowed *PrimeTime* to talk to or film Josh at all. I regretted not having protected him more.

And right in the middle of me having all these doubts about the wisdom of my action, the phone rang. It was 7:55 in the morning. I answered on the first ring so it wouldn't wake Barry or Josh.

It was a story editor from the syndicated magazine show *American Journal.* They were interested in doing an interview, for which I would be paid. And they agreed not to show Josh's face and to make him only a small part of the piece.

Some people close to me expressed the opinion that I was selling out. That I shouldn't profit from the tragedy, and I understood their point.

But they didn't understand the financial realities of the situation. I was a single parent who was head of the household and who was not able to return to work. I worked on commission and I was no longer able to do my job. I had no income and I didn't know when I'd have another check coming in. I had the FBI and the media to deal with, and I was the sole provider for Josh.

I also knew that if he was ever going to come to terms with the trauma, he would need a therapist, and that was going to be expensive. He was already having nightmares and trouble sleeping, and from time to time the rage he tried to keep inside would seep out and he'd explode. There was no quick fix. He was going to need lots of therapy, maybe even years of it if his dad was convicted.

Our lives had been interrupted and I faced two choices. I could sit back and let America hear me tell my story and answer questions for Diane Sawyer for nothing, or I could tell the same story to Nancy Glass and *American Journal* and be compensated. Not a difficult decision.

The sticking point was, one of the conditions of the *American Journal* contract was exclusivity and a first-run interview, which meant if *PrimeTime* aired their piece first, the deal with *AJ* was void.

I called Jamie Zahn at *PrimeTime* to discuss them pulling or delaying the piece and met some fierce resistance.

"What aren't you comfortable with, Lana?" she asked. "The piece is being edited today and is scheduled to be the lead segment on our Wednesday program."

"Please just pull it," I pleaded, not wanting to tell them about the *American Journal* contract. "Diane gave me her word she would hold it if I asked her." I wasn't very good at being devious, so in the end I simply told her why it was necessary.

"I have a chance to do a piece with *American Journal*," I said, "and if your program airs first, the deal is off. This is important to me because they're going to compensate us and I am really in a financial crunch."

My admission changed the entire tone of the conversation. In a heartbeat Jamie Zahn went from good-natured cajolery, trying to assuage my fears and get me to relent, to a hard-as-nails businesswoman fighting for a story.

"I'll talk to Diane," she said without sounding hopeful. "But you've got to understand. This is a news story, and it's our story. You're asking us to take a backseat and I don't see us doing it. The whole purpose of us coming out there was to get the story first."

So much for wanting to give me the opportunity to say my piece to the people of Oklahoma City and America, and that this ethical consideration was more important than anything else.

"What about Diane's promise?" I asked.

"She meant if your safety or Josh's safety were a factor. Not because you want to peddle your story to someone else." So now I was peddling it. . . .

The conversation with Sawyer herself was much the same. She took the soft, smooth-talking approach first, then, when I remained firm, she showed her resolve.

"You know we have the right to air this," she said strongly. "No one held a gun to your head to do this. You did it willingly. You're a big girl, Lana. You have to know that anytime you sit down with a reporter, especially in front of a camera, you are consenting to an interview. Now you want me to back off and give it up so another program can do it first. That wouldn't be prudent."

"You said you cared about us! About our well-being. About us surviving this."

"I do," she said weakly.

"Then understand, it's nothing personal. To make it for the next couple months, we really need the money they're going to pay us. We have no money coming in."

"And you didn't know this when we did the piece three days ago?"

"I'm sorry, I didn't." And that was the truth.

Sawyer was silent for a moment, then: "I'll discuss it with my producers, but no promises. And how long would you want us to delay airing it?"

"Just a week. You could air it on next Wednesday's show." I knew *American Journal* planned to bring a crew to Vegas to film on Saturday and have the interview on the air the following Monday, two days before *PrimeTime* was scheduled to air again.

Everyone at *PrimeTime* was passing the buck. They wanted to keep me happy, and not have to deal with the adverse publicity of a lawsuit, but they also wanted their top story. They had a dilemma.

"We'll get back to you as soon as we can," was the word from Jamie Zahn. "Our executive producer will make the final decision."

Hoping *PrimeTime* would let me off the hook, I agreed to a contract with *American Journal*. All of the back-and-forth phone calls had made for a tension filled day. I knew there was a reason I hated Mondays.

TUESDAY, MAY 2, 1995

A muscular FedEx courier appeared at my door a little after 10:00 A.M. with the contract from *American Journal*. I signed the agreement and drove it to the FedEx office on Eastern Avenue, where I sent it back priority overnight. They had enclosed a pre-filled-out air bill complete with their account number. Easy enough.

Then I went home and crossed my fingers, praying *PrimeTime* would call and agree to hold their program.

When the mail arrived at noon, Josh had a letter from Terry. It was handprinted, as was his style. He was excited to hear from his dad, and even more elated to learn that Terry would call him the following night at six o'clock. Nevada time.

Then the best news of the day.

A call from the executive producer of *PrimeTime Live*. It had taken two days, about nine phone calls, and the threat of a lawsuit, but they were giving in.

"We're going to hold the program," she said sharply. "We really don't have to and I think you know that. It's a good thing for you Diane Sawyer is so compassionate." McCurdy also tried to run a guilt trip on me, asking if I realized what a huge favor they were doing for me.

Thank you, thank you, thank you. *PrimeTime* had some class after all.

WEDNESDAY, MAY 3,1995

The normal reporter calls.

The Associated Press wanting to know if I had a comment about the latest FBI report that a receipt for the purchase of a ton of ammonium nitrate, bearing the fingerprints of accused bomber Timothy McVeigh, was discovered at Terry's Herington, Kansas, house.

Officials had verified that the receipt was issued by a Kansas fertilizer dealer. Federal agents had discovered blasting caps and blue plastic barrels at Terry's residence in a previous search.

Authorities had generally agreed that the explosion that destroyed the Murrah Federal Building was detonated by a 4,800-pound bomb composed of ammonium nitrate and fuel oil transported to the site in the Ryder truck and stored in 55-gallon barrels.

Experts had estimated that there had been at least twenty of the huge barrels in the truck and had found shards from the blue barrels in the debris. They did not believe one man could have mixed and loaded the bomb alone.

I had no comment.

Terry called promptly at 6:00 P.M. I accepted the charges on the collect call and spoke to him for a minute or so, just making small talk and inquiring about his health. I asked if he needed me to do anything about his house in Herington. I knew Marife was in protective custody and was being questioned, so there was no one at his house.

"I'd appreciate it if you had the utilities shut off," Terry said in a voice that told me he had made a list of all the things he needed done, but was too bashful to ask. Most of them I had to pry out of him, including the amount of his payment.

"My payment is $242," he said meekly. Terry was one of the most frugal men I'd ever met. He never wasted money and refused to spend even a buck if he thought something was overpriced.

All the time I was talking to Terry, Josh was pawing at me, anxious to grab the handset.

Their conversation was choppy and emotional. Terry had started to break down a bit when I was speaking to him.

"Dad, why is all this happening?" Josh asked, and began to bawl. Tears welled up in my eyes also. I could feel Josh's hurt, his loneliness, and his despair. All week he had been the man of the house, bearing up well under the pressure, but hearing his dad's voice turned him back into the little boy he really was. A scared little boy.

"I don't know, son," Terry replied. "I hope they'll get it all sorted out soon."

"Will I be able to visit you?"

"Not for a while, I'm afraid," and suddenly they were both crying at the same time.

I went in my bedroom and picked up the extension.

"Terry? It's Lana." He was openly sobbing and it got to me. "Are you eating okay?" He had been known to fast for days in the past, drinking only juices or water, just to cleanse his body of toxins. While I was in seclusion, the FBI had arranged for me to speak to Marife and she had expressed concern that Terry might try to starve himself as a form of protest.

"I'm okay," he said through teary gulps.

"Are you able to exercise or do anything?" Josh asked.

"Not really," he answered. "Maybe later."

"Are they treating you okay, Dad?"

"I guess. You know the government isn't going to give any special benefits to someone accused of a major crime."

"How often are you allowed to call?"

"Right now just once a week, and only for twenty minutes. So we're getting to that time."

"Will they give us a warning?" I asked.

"I don't know."

"I miss you, Dad. I love you, Dad."

"I love you, too, Josh. Keep your chin up. And write me a letter. My address is on the letter I sent you, although it will change if they transfer me to Oklahoma."

"I see where your lawyer is fighting that," I said.

"Yeah, but I don't think he can win."

"Dad . . ."

The phone went dead.

Josh kept yelling "I love you, Dad" into the buzzing receiver, his sobs drowning out everything around. It tore my guts out. I had never seen him hurt so much. He went into his room and didn't come out the rest of the night.

THURSDAY, MAY 4, 1995

The day started as it usually did, with a call from the *Washington Post,* followed by a call from a reporter at the *Daily Oklahoman.*

The New York Times had published a story suggesting that Tim and Terry might have been involved in a series of bank robberies in the Midwest over the past couple years. The paper cited a number of unsolved heists pulled off by a pair of Caucasian men using small pipe bombs. Terry and Tim fit the general descriptions of the perpetrators.

It was the first I'd heard about any bank robberies, but the wigs, masks, and panty hose I had found in the storage shed on Boulder Highway came immediately to mind. Was there a connection?

A story editor from *American Journal* called to let me know Kathy Difede Johnson, a segment producer and Nancy Glass's top aide, would be arriving in Las Vegas at 10:30. She would call to arrange meeting me so she could get some background material for the interview, and also planned to shoot some stock footage around my house and neighborhood.

Johnson turned out to be a bright, dark-haired woman in her early thirties. She was personable and confident and made Josh and me feel at ease very quickly.

She was familiar with the story, apparently having done her homework on the plane from Philadelphia. She was friendly with Josh, calling him "Joshua," and conveyed to him that she identified with the loss he was feeling over his dad.

I'm sure it made Josh feel a little better.

"When is Nancy Glass going to be in?" he asked when she was seated at our kitchen table.

"Nancy will be here Saturday morning," she replied. "She's got some shows to finish today and tomorrow in New York. I believe she's going to catch an early-morning flight and be in by eleven o'clock Saturday morning."

"Is that when you're going to do the taping?"

"Right. And I understand we're going to do it at a friend's house?"

"Yes. We have a friend named Andy who lives a few blocks away," I interjected. "We thought it would be easier to do it there. He has a little more room and we can keep the media away."

"That's probably a good idea," she agreed. "Sometimes the press can be a bit pushy and overbearing, especially when we're chasing a story this big."

Her talking about reporters and the aggressiveness of the media reminded me of a story I'd read a few days before in connection with Oklahoma City. The story claimed tabloid journalists from both TV and print had gone so far as to dress up like priests and firemen in order to gain access and get footage or stories inside the police lines surrounding the Murrah Building.

Some people may have seen it as enterprising, but I found it pathetic and distasteful.

"You're going to love Nancy," Johnson continued. "She's really special."

FRIDAY, MAY 5, 1995

The early morning was routine. A few calls from former coworkers in Michigan, a reporter or two, and a carpet-cleaning guy who had been trying to get through for a couple days without success.

Chuck Roberts, AFLAC insurance state coordinator and my old boss, called to see how we were doing. He, like another caller, Sandy Dasky, had been a friend to both Terry and me, and we had kept in touch over the years. Sandy was also an AFLAC agent in Michigan and was extremely successful.

It was nice to hear from them and to know they supported us.

"If you need anything, don't hesitate to call," Roberts offered.

The next call was not so pleasant. It was Director Prillaman.

"Lana, I'd like to send Agent Hawken out to your house if you don't mind. He has some pictures I'd like Josh to look at and he also has a copy of the subpoena from Oklahoma City.

"They want you to go to Oklahoma City next week, on Monday the eighth. Of course we'll make arrangements for your ticket and hotel."

As a rule, I try not to be nervous, but I am. I really was going to have to come face-to-face with Oklahoma City in just three days away. Prillaman told me agent Debbie Calhoun would be traveling with me.

When I asked if I needed a lawyer, he said it was my choice, but I might want to wait. He reminded me that I wasn't a suspect and that I was traveling to Oklahoma as a friendly witness. He also said if I changed my mind the U.S. attorney's office in Oklahoma City could and would provide counsel if I requested it. At no charge.

That was god to know because I imagined it would cost a lot to hire a good attorney. I wondered if Terry had competent legal counsel or if he was going to be stuck with some two-bit hack the court appointed.

"Will Josh have to go?" It was a question I was almost too scared to ask.

"The subpoena does not ask for him, so it isn't

necessary," Prillaman replied. That, at least, was good news. Josh didn't need the additional aggravation.

News of the subpoena meant the other shoe had dropped. With a thud. Prillaman had warned me it was coming, but now it was here. It was official. I was going to be a witness before the grand jury. While I wanted to do whatever was right, I didn't want to say things that would be detrimental to Terry. I felt boxed in.

I also felt angry. Angry at Terry for getting himself and us in to this situation. Even if he was innocent, it was because of him and his friends and his lifestyle that Josh and I were being forced to go through all this exhausting madness.

For Josh's sake, I had to maintain my equanimity. I couldn't let him see I was angry at his dad. It would have turned him against me and made him feel all alone. Right now, whether he knew it or not, I was all he had.

That was a new feeling for both of us, because in the past he'd always had his dad to go rock climbing with, or fishing or any of a dozen other activities they'd shared. I couldn't see myself doing those things.

I guess, in a way, I didn't know how to be a parent and companion to Josh at the same time. In many ways, Terry was more the nurturer to Josh than I was. I was his mother, but I worked outside the home and had grown accustomed to having my own space. And I needed it.

The *American Journal* interview was going to happen tomorrow and I didn't have any idea about what I was going to say. I'd just answer their questions and try not to get myself in trouble.

I knew the FBI wasn't thrilled about the television and newspaper exposure I was getting. They probably cringed every time they saw my name in the paper or heard I was going to be on television.

But they hadn't told me not to talk. No gag order. Besides, if I had any information that was really secret or vital to the case, they would have put me undercover.

The last call I had on Friday evening was from Bob Macy of the Associated Press in Las Vegas.

Somehow he had been tipped about the fact that I had been served with a subpoena. Macy was an old pro with a gentle approach and I was putty in his hands. I admitted that I had been subpoenaed but managed to avoid giving him the exact date of my departure.

SATURDAY, MAY 6, 1995

This would eventually prove to be one of the most unbelievable days of Josh's and my life, and when I look back I can see it was the most climactic and stressful of any during the entire proceedings. It would shape our destiny, change the nature of our relationship with the FBI, brand me as a a loose-lipped, over protective mother and Josh as a possible material witness.

It started with a banner headline in the *Las Vegas Review-Journal* that announced, NICHOLS' EX-WIFE TO TESTIFY BEFORE GRAND JURY. My two-minute interview with the Associated Press the previous night had been transformed into a major story.

The only question I hadn't answered was whether or not I'd met Timothy McVeigh. As I said, I did not reveal when I was going to Oklahoma City and told Bob Macy that I honestly didn't know exactly when I would testify.

Macy had also asked if Josh was going to testify.

"Absolutely not," I had replied, raising my voice.

The body count in Oklahoma City had risen to 167, with hundreds more injured. Pictures of the building were horrifying and the structural damage was so severe that plans were already in the works to level the entire edifice by implosion. The city's downtown section had been declared a disaster area by Oklahoma governor Frank Keating.

I wasn't looking forward to going there. I knew the people of the city were justifiably hostile and I didn't know what the mood would be toward me.

I scanned the paper and found a couple more stories about the bombing.

OKBomb was the code name assigned to the case by the FBI, and seventeen days after the blast, rescue workers were still finding bodies and body parts. A story out of Oklahoma claimed "all the bodies may never be found."

It was 7:30 A.M. and I was at my kitchen table reading the paper and sipping my first cup of coffee.

At eight, Kathy Johnson called. "Hope I didn't wake you," she answered.

"You didn't. You forget, I'm a country girl at heart. If I were still in Michigan, I would have milked the cows and plowed a field by now.

She got right to the point. "I just wanted to let you know Nancy will be in at eleven, but we'd like to get over to your friend's house and set up at least an hour ahead. I have the address, so we could just meet you and Josh there around ten if that works for you."

"That will be fine. We'll see you there."

It took more than an hour just to set up the lights and monitors, get the sound level where they wanted it, and move some household plants and fixtures around to create the proper background.

While the crew was buzzing about doing the technical stuff, Johnson was chatting with me, trying to learn as much as she could about Josh and me and our emotional state.

"It varies moment to moment," I said not exaggerating. "It would be nice if we could just get in sync with our moods. I mean, if Josh could be sad when I'm strong, and vice-versa. That way we could prop each other up."

She took pages and pages of notes in order to brief Glass and allow her to focus on the highlights of the story.

By the time Nancy Glass arrived at noon, the crew was about ready to shoot.

"Hi, I'm Nancy Glass," she said, offering her hand. She was tall and willowy, with a slight frame, and appeared much thinner in person than she did on TV. "You must be Lana."

I liked her instantly. There was a warmth about her that couldn't be faked. And she listened. It made for a better interview because many of her questions developed from things I told her in general conversation just minutes before the cameras began to roll.

No matter how long someone guesstimates a shooting will take, you can add an extra hour or two, and this was no exception.

Johnson had estimated the shoot would go from noon until about 2:30. I think she knew better but just didn't want to get Josh and me all worked up. It went well, and we filmed both inside and out rather efficiently. Despite this, it still took three hours and forty-five minutes.

For the most part the interview was serious, but there was one cute incident involving Nancy and Josh that I'm sure will wind up in a TV bloopers or outtakes show.

We had agreed that she could ask Josh a couple of questions, provided that his face was distorted or digitized when the interview was aired. That way the audience would hear his voice and see his body but not his face. This portion was shot in the driveway, with Nancy in the street facing the house and Josh in the driveway. The cameraman tried to focus on Nancy and set the camera to shoot over Josh's shoulder. Problem was Josh, who is five-eight, towered over five-six Nancy, and what with the slope of the driveway, she wasn't visible in the shot.

So they improvised. A milk crate was located and the shot came off with Glass standing on the "soapbox" to interview a twelve-year-old. The crate, of course, wasn't visible to the audience when the show aired, but the camera guys couldn't resist taking some long-range shots just for fun.

When the interview was over, we shot a few still shots as souvenirs and went our separate ways. Josh was anxious to get home, Nancy and Kathy had a plane to catch, and I was looking forward to lying out in the backyard to grab some rays from the still-warm afternoon sun.

Nice thoughts. No chance.

Josh and I buzzed the few blocks home silently. He had cooperated and seemed to like Nancy, but I had the feeling he was hiding behind some sort of emotional shield. There was no way he could be immune to the news, the newspapers, and the pressure.

We were home in three minutes. Barry was in the front yard mowing the lawn, and he came alongside the driver's side of the car even before I could shut the engine off.

"You had a message from the FBI," he said. "Agent Calhoun called twice. She asked for you to call her back as soon as you got here."

It was 3:50.

Debbie Calhoun wanted Josh and me to come down to the FBI office ASAP.

"I'm really sorry to have to ask you to come down at this time on a Saturday afternoon," she said apologetically when we arrived. "But it's really important.

"There have been some critical new developments and we need to interview Josh again to see if he can help fill in some gaps. If you can have someone drop you off, we'll arrange for an agent to get you back home as soon as we're finished."

Neither of us wanted to go. Josh was outside playing basketball with his friends Carmine and Mike, and the pool was still beckoning to me.

Josh balked as I expected.

"C'mon," I said, trying to lighten things up and entice him. "We'll probably be in and out of there in a flash. I'm sure all the agents want to go home, too."

And then, for some insurance: "If we get going now, we'll stop and get a milkshake and go to the card shop on the way home." Josh had recently developed a passion for sports cards and player autographs, and I was glad to see him take an interest in something constructive, even though it was an expensive hobby.

Recently he had acquired autographed 8x10s of his favorite football players, Barry Sanders and Drew Bledsoe, and he showed them off whenever we had visitors.

"You know we're not going to be able to get in and out of there fast," he argued. "It always takes a long time."

"Not today," I said, hoping I wasn't lying to him. "We won't let them keep us. Besides, they're going to tell us some of the things your dad said when he turned himself in. I'm sure you're interested in that."

That was the motivation he needed. Any chance he had to learn more about his dad's situation piqued his interest. He had even asked one of the agents about the size of Terry's cell and did they open his mail. He was hungry for any scrap of information. Terry was still his idol.

Barry drove us to the FBI building in my car and Josh stood and watched the street long after his brother had pulled out of the parking lot and disappeared down Charleston Boulevard. It was just another sign of his reluctance. Because it was so late in the afternoon, I expected to be able to get in and out of the FBI building in a flash.

I was never more wrong, and the date, May 6, 1995, will be indelibly burned into my brain for the rest of my life. It was a sweet-and-sour day. *American Journal* in the morning and early afternoon, and the FBI from four o'clock to 10:30 P.M.

We were there six and a half hours, and when we left we were both drained, battered wrecks.

The Vegas FBI offices have lots of little rooms. Most, like the fingerprint room, the records room, and the mug-shot room are designed for specific purposes. Having spent many hours in the bureau, Josh and I were familiar with most of them. The one we had found ourselves in today had a time line taped to the wall outlining statements made by Josh, Marife, Terry, and Tim.

In the beginning, the questioning was of a general nature, with the agents trying to get Josh and me to fill in the missing parts to the time line.

They repeatedly asked about the time Josh's flight left Kansas, and why he flew from Kansas City instead of Wichita. Kansas City was a hundred miles farther from Herington, so it didn't seem logical to them.

They thought it might have been Terry's idea.

"It was cheaper from Kansas City," I explained. "And I was paying for the ticket."

"What airline did Josh fly on?"

"Southwest. I got the ticket thirty days in advance so we could get a discount fare. I always tried to plan his trips and get the tickets early to get the cheaper fare."

"Did you speak to Terry that night?"

"He called from the airport to tell me Josh was on his way. I think that was around eleven o'clock Kansas time. Josh arrived in Las Vegas around one-fifteen or one-thirty in the morning on the eighteenth." I couldn't remember the exact time.

"Did Terry say anything else?"

"Like what?"

"Discuss anything, other than the fact Josh was on the plane."

"I could only assume he was going home. It was late and he had Marife and the baby with him."

Little did I know that in the months to come, the FBI

would confiscate the phone records of all the phone booths at Kansas City International Airport until they came up with the exact phone Terry had used to call me. By scouring the log from that phone, they traced the calls he made just before the call to me, and the ones he made just after.

The calls before turned out to have no significance. But the very next call after Terry called me was placed to Tim McVeigh. What a coincidence.

Again the conversation shifted to the time line and the statements on the wall. Josh's comments from previous interviews were in white; things Terry had said to the authorities in Kansas were in green. Marife's recollection of the events and actions of the parties involved over the week preceding the bombing were in pink. Tim's statement line, which was blank except for his comment about being a prisoner of war and the time of his arrest, was in yellow.

The statements were aligned horizontally across the wall, and as near as I could tell, the accounts given by Josh, Terry, and Marife all seemed to be consistent.

I glanced at the clock. It was straight up six o'clock. We had already been there for two hours.

Meanwhile, Josh was asking more questions about his dad.

Who decided if he got bail? How long could they hold him? Could he talk to him? Could he visit him?

"No. Not yet. You can't visit him yet and there will be a hearing on the bail real soon." There was talk of Terry being transferred to jail in Oklahoma. If that happened, then maybe a visit could be arranged for Josh.

Agent Dick MacArthur showed Josh pictures of rescuers sifting through the rubble. "They've found the axle to the truck which carried the bomb," he said with assurance. "Josh, they're going to find the rest of that truck, and when they do, we'll be able to identify the fingerprints.

"If you were in that Ryder truck or were there when it was rented, you might as well tell me now because we're going to find out. I want you to understand you're not a target or a suspect. We know you didn't do anything wrong. We only want you to tell us the truth."

"I've already told you I wasn't there." Josh was rightfully agitated. I understood the FBI guys were just doing their job, but they were badgering him.

"Let's go and get a Coke," Agent MacArthur suggested, and Josh quickly accepted the chance to interrupt the questioning.

"I want you to have a look at something," Debbie Calhoun said to me as soon as Josh and Agent MacArthur were out of sight.

It was now after 8:00 P.M., and even though the questioning sessions had been taxing, we had been given lots of rest breaks. It wasn't like they were at us every minute.

Agent Calhoun laid two pictures on the table. One was the sketch of John Doe #2; the one next to it was a mug shot of Josh.

"Where did you get that picture of Josh?" I immediately demanded.

"We took it here in the office last week," Calhoun said. "We were showing Josh some of the different sections to the office, and when we got to the photo area, he asked us to take his picture. He also asked us to fingerprint him."

She reached for her briefcase and brought up a large red-and-white index-style card. "Here is his fingerprint sheet," she said, handing it to me. "You may keep it if you like."

I stared silently at the pictures for a few seconds.

"Do you see a resemblance?" she pressed.

The longer I stared, the more the pictures started to blend together.

"I think Josh could be our John Doe two," Calhoun

Lana with baby Josh in 1983

A happy family—Lana, Terry, Josh, Barry,
and a Swedish exchange student

The Nichols men—Terry, father Robert, brother James, and Terry's son Josh in 1984

Terry Nichols clowning for the camera in 1986

The house in Decker, Michigan, where Terry, Lana, and Josh lived from 1987 to 1991

Terry and Josh with a baby fawn they found in their garden on the farm in Decker, Michigan in 1987

Josh, the little outdoorsman, holding a rifle, 1989

Lana and son Josh in 1987

Terry Nichols
in camouflage
in 1989

Terry and
second wife,
Marife, on
their wedding
day in 1990

Terry, Marife, and Josh celebrating Josh's ninth birthday in 1991

Timothy McVeigh holding Terry and Marife's son Jason, who later died mysteriously

Terry and Marife's son Jason shortly before his death in 1993

Terry, Timothy McVeigh, and Josh on vacation at Niagara Falls in 1992

Lana and Josh celebrating his thirteenth birthday,
August 1995

Lana, Josh, and author Ron Delpit in August 1995

said bluntly. The tone of her voice told me she wasn't joking. "I think he's either denying it because he doesn't want to implicate his father, or because he doesn't want to be in trouble himself. It makes sense," she continued, trying to sell me on the idea.

"He was there. He's the right size. And if he was wearing dark clothing or the clerk saw him from a distance, his build could easily be mistaken for an older man's.

"And we know Terry and McVeigh are comfortable with Josh around. . . ." Debbie Calhoun's voice trailed off, and I kept my eyes on the pictures, following from one to another as if I was watching the ball at a tennis match.

The harder I looked, the more I could see of Josh in the John Doe #2 sketch. I was getting sick to my stomach.

Just then Josh and Agent MacArthur sauntered back in.

I called Josh over.

"Look at these pictures, Josh. In this shot you do look a lot like John Doe number two," I said guardedly.

"I think you were there," Agent Calhoun said pointedly. She was buoyed by my having taken the lead.

"I was there. I'm John Doe number two," Josh responded. He waited a count or two for all of our jaws to drop, then added, "Just kidding."

Josh chuckled when he said it, but he did it like a kid who had let something slip and was trying to cover it up before an adult got angry.

What was the truth?

The questioning intensified a little over the next hour, with the agents playing good cop, bad cop with Josh. One would try to gain his confidence by being pals with him while the other would tell him his cooperation could help his father.

"If my dad told you what he knows, would they make him a deal?" he asked at one juncture. It made the investigator sit up quickly.

"It certainly could," came the reply. But there was no further comment forthcoming from Josh.

It was after ten o'clock by now and I could see Josh's energy level was nearing zero. His tolerance level was about the same. He got up and went to the bathroom.

When he returned, it was to a chair in the corner of the room with a couple agents hovered around him.

"Just a couple more things and we'll be done." It was Agent Debbie Calhoun's ball now. It was her theory that Josh was John Doe #2 and she was intent on riding it out. She went back to that line of questioning.

Suddenly Josh stood up, turned to the wall, and folded his arms. "I don't want to talk anymore," he announced. "I'll only talk to my dad."

They hadn't broken him, but it was obvious he had had enough. Josh's adamant stance concerned me. Had he just had all he could take or was he protecting himself or his dad? He was loyal and devoted to Terry. And maybe brainwashed a little.

"You know, he could be arrested as a material witness," Agent Calhoun said, looking in my direction.

"Arrest a twelve-year-old kid! Over my dead body," I screamed. I was getting a bit hysterical.

Josh was upset. He was non-communicative and I could see he was breathing hard. He was flexing his shoulders and back as he inhaled and exhaled rapidly. He was still facing the wall with his arms folded across his chest in a defiant posture.

Was he really John Doe #2? Did he know who John Doe #2 was? I was confused but it didn't matter. I wasn't going to let them take Josh away.

I didn't know I was crying until one of the agents handed me a handkerchief. I took it without looking up.

"He seems to be really upset," Director Prillaman said calmly. "Maybe it would be best if we arranged for him to go to Charter Hospital for the night, or a couple days. That way someone could keep an eye on him to be sure he didn't try to run away or do something to himself."

I think he was trying to be helpful. I know through it all he was a gentleman and all of the agents in Las Vegas had our best interests and safety at heart. But this was too much. Charter Hospital!

Then, in a softer, almost whispery voice an agent made the most dangerous suggestion I think I've ever heard.

"Josh may subconsciously be trying to block out certain memories of that week," he said. "Maybe if we were allowed to hypnotize him, he'd be able to remember."

Hypnotize him. Were they nuts? Goose bumps were running up my arms and back. Obviously the FBI and the government would go to any lengths to solve this case. Risking permanent damage to a twelve-year-old boy was a casualty they could live with. *Sorry if he's been traumatized, Mrs. Padilla. It was all in the interest of national security.*

I wanted to vomit.

"He'll be okay once we get home," I said, sounding a little calmer. "Just take us home." No one argued.

My insides were vibrating like a pinball machine.

Josh's outburst had effectively ended the interview for the evening and we were whisked home without another question being asked. My muscles ached and my head was splitting.

Suddenly nothing was clear. Maybe I had more to worry about than Terry. I was divorced from him. I couldn't bear to lose Josh. What the hell had Terry gotten him into?

As we got out of the FBI car in front of our house I was sure of only one thing. No matter how friendly the FBI people had been up to this point, if they felt either Josh or myself was withholding something, they would squash us like bugs. I had no illusions about that.

Not in this case. Not with the public outcry and the political pressure to capture the bad guys no matter what it took. In that way it was like the Simpson case, but as one FBI agent said, "Before it's all over, this case will make the Simpson case look like a fight over a parking ticket."

We needed a lawyer and a very good one—fast—or we might be going down for the count.

6

FINDING A GOOD LAWYER IS NEVER EASY.
Reaching that same lawyer on a Sunday morning is about
as likely as winning the lottery. Without a ticket.

And how much would it cost?

We didn't need Perry Mason or Matlock. We weren't
criminals; we only needed guidance. If they were going to
seriously consider Josh as John Doe #2 and threaten to
arrest him as a material witness I wanted to know our
rights.

MAY 7, 1995

My friend Andy, who makes a living as a magazine writer,
suggested two powerful local attorneys and agreed to
contact them on our behalf.

"Do you think you can get them on Sunday?" I asked
skeptically.

"People get arrested on Sunday," he kidded. "I'll try
and reach them at home."

I resisted asking what they charged because I couldn't
put a price tag on our freedom, or more accurately, on
Josh's rights and freedom. The FBI wasn't threatening
me. Yet. Even though I had to assume that might be the
next step. Perhaps they'd try to implicate me in some way
because of the letters.

I certainly didn't need this to happen the day before I was scheduled to travel to Oklahoma to meet with the grand jury. I was nervous enough. What was the jury going to ask? What was I going to say? I alternated between feeling confident and scared out of my wits. I felt like a very small fish in a very large, very nightmarish bowl. Why was everything so crazy and out of control?

It'll never stop, I thought, and suddenly I was crying again.

Despite having three phone numbers for him, Andy tried unsuccessfully to contact Stan Hunterton, who was the personal attorney of the owner of the Mirage Hotel, Steve Wynn. Hunterton was apparently out of town for the weekend, which meant he couldn't help us. I needed someone now. Like five minutes ago.

He did manage to reach Kent Devereaux (not his real name), one of the best-known criminal attorneys in the city and one of Andy's former weekend basketball buddies. Devereaux was second in command at one of the most powerful firms in the city and had recently gotten some national recognition for winning a seemingly unwinnable drug case.

Legend had it his firm had once had a sodomy charge reduced to tailgating—no pun intended—then to "following too closely" before having it dismissed altogether.

Andy said the good news was that these lawyers were very, very clever and seldom lost a case, no matter what the odds. The bad news was they were very expensive, and the government was their mortal enemy. I wasn't sure I wanted to take an adversarial position with the United States of America and the FBI, but at the moment I didn't feel I had a choice.

As it turned out, Kent Devereaux was familiar with the case, having followed it in the local papers and on the news. Initially he wanted to meet at his office in downtown Las Vegas, but the ongoing press patrol outside my front door, coupled with the fact that the FBI had stationed agents in surveillance cars at each end of the block, called for a different arrangement.

We were beginning to depend on Andy a lot more, as a friend, and as an adviser. Josh and I both trusted him and he had demonstrated a genuine interest in helping us. Also, Josh liked him a lot. Josh was able to talk to him or kid around with him and he always seemed to have time to listen.

After a short conversation, Andy gave Devereaux directions to our house. The mountain was coming to Mohammad.

Kent Devereaux arrived in the early afternoon. He was a rangy, nice-looking man in his late thirties, and his style, at least at the moment, was casual. Dressed in dark brown cowboy boots, beige Docker pants, and an open-necked white shirt, he looked more like a vacationing software executive than a barracuda attorney from the high-rent district.

When Devereaux spoke, however, he took charge, and he was all business.

"You definitely need a lawyer," he said flatly when I had finished recounting the Saturday-night ordeal at the FBI building. "You should have had one weeks ago, when the FBI first showed up at your office. It would have saved you a lot of heartaches."

I offered him coffee, and while I was in the kitchen preparing it, he asked Andy quietly about our ability to pay his fee. Andy told him we could not afford his normal $10,000 retainer. Nor could we pay a $5,000 fee.

"Can they come up with a thousand?"

Andy told him we could handle that, and when I returned to the room, Devereaux cut right to the chase.

"I'll represent Josh, but not you," he announced. "I don't think you need me right now. You're already cooperating and have not resisted the subpoena. You're considered a friendly witness. Josh would not be. Not if they would expect him to testify against his father. You'll testify at the grand jury hearing tomorrow and basically be done with it.

"If they have this wild hair that Josh is John Doe number two, they're not going to back off. With an attorney, they can't contact him directly. The harassment will stop immediately. If the FBI calls, just tell them you have a lawyer and to contact my office. They certainly know who I am.

"I suppose Andy has told you that I am not a particular favorite of the FBI. They respect me, but they don't like me, which is okay. They don't have to like me. I've made them look bad and beaten them in court a number of times."

It was easy to see Kent Devereaux relished the high-profile nature of the case. And while the fee was more than reasonable, it concerned me that he might have a mixed agenda. The reams of publicity and additional notoriety Devereaux would get was okay by me, and I realized it came with the territory. I just wanted to be sure Josh's well-being was his primary concern and that my son's rights were not compromised.

I brought Devereaux up to date on my difficulties in negotiating with *PrimeTime* to delay airing their piece, told him about the *American Journal* segment, which was scheduled to air the following night, and tried as best I could to summarize the numerous sessions Josh and I had endured with the FBI.

"We were just trying to be helpful and answer whatever questions they had," I explained when I saw Devereaux frowning. His angular face was well tanned, and he wore glasses with round gold frames that he pushed up on his nose from time to time.

"I know what you were trying to do, Ms. Padilla, but you have to understand, the federal government doesn't give a damn about you. All they care about is solving this case and they will use anyone and anything they can to do it.

"This is the most important case any of these agents will see in their lifetimes.

"For that reason, I also suggest you be very cautious about what you say on the telephone, because you can pretty much assume it's tapped. Yours, too, Andy.

"As far as the television stuff, I wish you hadn't done it, but it's too late to change that.

"When is the *American Journal* segment due to run?"

"Tomorrow night," Josh said from the sofa, where he had been taking it all in.

"I'm not going to watch it," I said for no reason. "Besides, I'll be in Oklahoma tomorrow morning to testify before the grand jury. I've asked Andy to come with me and the FBI is sending a female agent to accompany me."

"You don't intend to take Josh, do you?" Devereaux asked.

"No."

"That's wise. Because if they wanted to be nasty about it, they could serve him with a material-witness warrant while you were there," Devereaux said seriously. "And what about the *PrimeTime* piece. When is that supposed to be on?"

"Wednesday," Andy responded.

"I expect you'll be in Oklahoma City tomorrow and Tuesday," Devereaux said. "I want to see you and Josh in my office as soon as you get back. Bring any paperwork you have at that time. And if anyone from the government or FBI calls, refer them to my office."

He gave us a card with his office and cellular number, then wrote his home number on the back.

"Don't hesitate to call me. For any reason," he emphasized. "In the meantime I'll try and contact the legal departments at *American Journal* and *PrimeTime* to make sure everybody is playing by the same rules."

A few minutes later I wrote out the check for a thousand dollars and Kent Devereaux folded it neatly and tucked it into his shirt pocket. Before leaving, he tried to comfort me.

"You can rest a little easier from here on out," he said. "You have some help now. Things are going to get better."

I doubt that he's ever been more wrong in his life.

Since Andy had been kind enough to introduce us to Devereaux, I hesitated about telling him that I still wasn't sold on the guy. His credentials were impeccable, and he had presented himself well, but there was something about him that left me feeling a bit uncomfortable. Since I couldn't put my finger on it, I let it slide.

MONDAY, MAY 8, 1995

I was anxious. I was up and down most of the night, finally settling on the couch at about four in the morning. At 5:30, I made coffee and called Andy. He was up and ready.

The plan was for him to pick me up at 6:00 A.M.. We were to meet Agent Calhoun at the Southwest departure gate at 6:30. The flight to Oklahoma City was scheduled to leave at 6:55.

We checked our bags with a curbside porter and headed for the C gate, which meant we would have to take the tram-style monorail to the Southwest area. It was a pleasant and incredibly quick twenty-second ride, so passengers seldom whined about the small inconvenience.

Agent Calhoun was there waiting, and as soon as she saw us approaching, she stood and moved toward us.

"Good morning, Lana."

"Good morning, Debbie. This is my friend Andy Donovan."

She barely acknowledged him.

"I've just been notified that our trip has been canceled," she said dryly. "I'm really sorry to have gotten you up and dragged you out here this time of morning." She didn't sound very sorry.

"Why? What happened?" I asked innocently.

"I don't know yet. I just got a call from the office that the trip was a 'no-go.' I won't know why until I get to the office. I'd guess the order came from Oklahoma. Maybe they weren't ready for you today. I'll call you at home as soon as they tell me when the trip has been rescheduled."

I was disappointed, and peeved. Disappointed because it had taken a lot for me to psych myself up to face the grand jury, and irritated because our bags were already checked and I was convinced there was more to the trip being aborted than Debbie Calhoun was saying.

Weeks later I would learn that my instincts had been correct. The trip was canceled because Andy had accompanied me. He was considered a "press" person and had made some statements to the media on our behalf during the past ten days. The FBI considered him an outsider and was none too thrilled with his input. They certainly didn't want him being privy to any of the goings-on in Oklahoma.

Rather than waste our early start, Andy and I waited patiently while the ticket agent retrieved our bags, then we went to breakfast and planned the day's strategy.

Instead of waiting until Wednesday, I'd get Josh up and we'd go downtown to Devereaux's office as soon as he could see us.

Devereaux's second-floor offices were spacious and tastefully decorated with a large atrium area in the middle of a suite of offices and conference rooms. His office was large, with a vintage pinball machine in one corner and various UNLV Runnin' Rebel basketball paraphernalia in the other. Miscellaneous newspaper clippings and law degrees decorated the walls.

Devereaux welcomed us warmly, and was not surprised to hear about our trip being canceled.

"I'm willing to bet your friend was the reason," he surmised. "They might figure he's going to write an 'insider' type article and reveal certain things they consider sensitive. This case has so much heat on it no one wants to screw up.

"I've already spoken to the U.S. attorney in Oklahoma City," he continued, "and I've got a call in to the special prosecutor. I want to find out just where they stand with Josh."

He looked at my subpoena and scanned some FBI receipts I had brought along. One was a carbon showing I had given them permission to go in and get papers or anything they deemed necessary for evidence while we were being sequestered at Circus-Circus. Another was a receipt for things they had confiscated from my house.

Most of it was Terry's property. They had taken everything from his army shooting trophies to letters and old family pictures. Anything that had any link to him. Now I wished I had been there, or someone had been there to watch them. To see what they took. As it was, I had just given them carte blanche to roam through my house. I was willing to bet they took full advantage of it.

To this day, I have not received everything on the invoice back, and whatever pictures there were of Tim and Terry together, the FBI kept.

"I'll put these in a file," the lawyer said, holding up the subpoena and other papers. "And as soon as someone from the government returns my call, I'll be in touch."

As Josh and I stood to leave Devereaux spoke again.

"You know, Lana, because of your involvement and the fact the information you have indicates you will be a prosecution witness, you might consider appointing a temporary guardian for Josh, someone else to make decisions about what he should do as far as cooperating, voluntarily testifying, or seeking immunity.

"Perhaps an attorney or someone else who understands all the ramifications and has no vested interest other than what's best for Josh."

It took a minute for what he said to register, but when it did, I was on fire inside. Here was someone else trying to take my kid away from me. First the FBI wants to put him in Charter Hospital and have a psychologist interrogate him. Maybe even hypnotize him. And now a darn lawyer I've known for five seconds wants to control him.

I was so mad I was afraid of what I might say, so I bit my tongue.

"I'm not sure that's a good idea," I finally said, proud of the fact I hadn't come unglued. "But I'll give it some thought." Bull. The only thing I would be giving thought to was whether or not I wanted to have Kent Devereaux continue to represent us. No one was going to take Josh away from me, and I could see that this might well become an issue down the road with Devereaux.

"By the way, Lana, I spoke to the people at *PrimeTime* regarding digitizing Josh's face and cutting out any parts that might be detrimental to him. I think I shook them up a little," Devereaux continued, apparently unaware of the molten lava coursing through my nervous system.

"They're very sensitive about lawsuits. We may be able to resolve it lawyer to lawyer. They have two days to reedit it since it doesn't run until Wednesday."

Andy met us outside the office and we decided Josh would go with him, which would give me some time to run a few errands.

As expected, two FBI cars followed the car in which Josh was riding.

Wherever Josh went, he had a silent entourage. The agents on the street were not concerned about the rest of us. Only Josh. If I went to the grocery store, no one followed. If Josh accompanied me, the two FBI cars would join us.

As we walked out of Devereaux's office the agents revved up their engines, ready to tail whichever car Josh entered. It wasn't a big deal because Director Prillaman had advised me they'd be following him, for his own protection.

On this Monday morning, their diligence proved both humorous and helpful, and the agents got more than they bargained for.

We desperately needed a new TV, the old one in our living room being a relic from the eighties, so I enlisted Josh and Andy to check out a couple of electronics discount stores instead of going directly home from the law offices.

Josh was demanding more and more attention and I could feel the underlying current of hostility growing inside him. We had seen a counselor, Joan Owen, and she had warned me to expect a change in his behavior and to prepare myself for his rage.

Sending him to the store to buy the TV would give me a chance to do a few things as well as occupy him for a short time. Without school, he was idle most of the day. It wasn't as if he could play with his friends because they were in class until 2:30. He was like a fish out of water.

Armed with money I had managed to scrape together from my kitchen emergency fund and a small insurance commission check, Josh and Andy headed for Ultimate Electronics with both FBI cars in their wake.

The agents waited patiently in their cars in the Ultimate parking lot while Josh and Andy browsed. Finding nothing to their liking, they got back in the car and headed for Circuit City, the agents once again right on their bumper.

Josh picked out a twenty-five-inch GE table model at the second store, but the box wouldn't fit in the car. Delivery would have taken a couple days and cost twenty-five dollars, but Josh had a better idea.

One of the agents was driving a Chevy Blazer and Josh spotted him about thirty yards away, facing the store's entrance. He unabashedly strolled over to the fed in the Blazer.

"Hey, I was wondering if you could do us a favor?" he asked.

The agent looked back blankly. He probably never expected to have Josh confront him like this.

"The TV we just bought won't fit in our car," Josh said. "What are the chances we could put it in your car? You *are* going back to my house when we go, aren't you?"

"I guess I could do that," the agent mumbled. He was too flabbergasted to refuse.

The man whipped his Blazer around to the entrance, shifted a few of his personal belongings to make room, and the warehouse clerk loaded the TV through the rear door.

When they got home, the agent helped unload the TV, then retreated to his post at the north end of the street.

Since the agents weren't working undercover, I guess what Josh had done was no big deal. And since the agents were not opposed to lending a hand, we used them on two other occasions as well.

One night Josh was bugging me to take him to a friend's house, but I didn't have my car. His pleading got so annoying I finally walked out into my driveway and signaled to the nearest agent.

The man drove up and rolled down his window.

"He wants to go to a friend's house and I don't have a car," I explained. "Would you mind taking him? I mean, if someone came to pick him up, you'd just have to follow him anyway. Right?"

Another time, after the FBI had confiscated Josh's shoes, which we later found out they had done in order to check them for traces of the chemicals that had been used in making the bomb, I asked one of the agents to take him to Foot Locker.

"You guys have his shoes," I said. "So I guess you should take him to get some new ones." I gave Josh my ATM card and told him to spend no more than eighty dollars.

A few minutes later my phone rang. It was the agent.

"The shoes he wants cost eighty-five dollars plus tax, Ms. Padilla. Do you still want him to get them?"

"It's okay. Whatever you guys don't reimburse, I'll pay the difference." The bureau had only authorized a fifty-five-dollar reimbursement. I guess they haven't been sneaker shopping lately.

Late in the afternoon Kent Devereaux called to report that he'd received a call from the FBI requesting that I gather all of the clothing Josh had taken when he went to visit his dad in Kansas.

"The order came from Oklahoma," he said.

"Do I have to do it?" I asked.

"We could fight it, but then they'd just get a formal court order."

I couldn't even remember all the things he'd taken. I'd packed some of it, he'd packed a few things, and we tossed some stuff in at the last minute.

"Why do they want his clothes anyway?" I demanded. "And what the hell is he supposed to wear in the meantime? Will they be giving them back?"

"They really didn't say why they wanted them, but my guess is they want to show them to the Ryder clerk to see if he recognizes anything. I'll call them about reimbursing you for replacement clothes, and I don't know if they'll be giving them back. I wouldn't count on it. If they think it's evidence of any kind, they'll hold on to it for however long they think necessary.

"Truthfully, Josh will outgrow them before he gets them back."

Great. Now he needed a new wardrobe, and I had to go rummaging through his closet and drawers to try to find what he'd taken to Kansas. I just shook my head and looked skyward. I needed God to give me strength.

What's more, with everything going on, there was no way I could concentrate at the office. My mond was on Josh, on the case, on the unanswered questions and the constant intrusion of the media.

Then I had my family to deal with. I hadn't heard from my sisters, nor had I heard from any of Terry's family. I had, however, spoken to my dad. I though it might be a good idea to call and let him know about the *American Journal* and *PrimeTime* interviews before they aired.

"I just wanted to let you know that I've spoken to the press," I told him after we exchanged uneasy hellos. "I just didn't want you to see it on television without me letting you know first."

He was livid.

"I can't believe you would go public, Lana. What's the matter with you? Why did you have to do that?"

"Because I can't just sit by and say nothing, and because they agreed to pay me. We need the money, too, Daddy. I have to support me and Josh. Who's going to pay our bills? Are you going to send me two thousand dollars a month so I can put food on the table and make my house payment? I didn't think so," I shouted when he didn't respond.

I was yelling and tears were streaming down my face. He didn't want to understand, and neither did he offer to pay my bills, even though he could have afforded to.

"But you have your own real-estate office. Isn't that enough to support you? You didn't have to go on television and make a spectacle of yourself."

It was useless trying to get through to him.

"I work on commission, Daddy. If I'm not out there selling houses, I don't get paid. There's so much happening I can't even go to my office. We're under a lot of pressure here."

"All I know is Terry couldn't have done this. Not Terry."

"I don't know what to think right now, Daddy. All I know is Josh and I are in the middle of all this and we're all alone."

"I still don't agree with you being on television. If you just kept quiet, they'd leave you alone. Don't say anything. The less you say the better, because this way you're going to drag the whole family into it. I don't want us all on the news."

"Is that all you care about—the news? The family being dragged down." I was screaming again. Arguments with my dad always touched my hot button. I always felt like a little girl being reprimanded. But I was forty-five years old and I wasn't going to take being scolded without a fight.

"I'm going to do what I have to do. I don't give a damn what anybody thinks!" I slammed the phone down. He was angry and so was I. We both had tempers and had clashed before.

The *American Journal* piece aired at 7:30 Vegas time on Monday night and I didn't watch it. Troy taped it so I could see it when I felt stronger.

Kent Devereaux did watch it, however, and when it was over he called, and I could tell he was in agony.

"I saw it," he responded when I asked. "I can understand why the FBI is going bonkers over you doing it. You've probably exposed at least half of their case. It really makes their job more difficult."

He hesitated, and I could tell he wanted to ask something else.

"Um . . . Could the *PrimeTime* piece be any more explosive?"

I hesitated as long in answering.

Finally, I said, "I think it is, because they talk to Josh a lot, and because I told them more about the letters and the package. I didn't know any better. I just rambled on. . . ."

I thought I heard him say "OmiGod," but I couldn't be sure.

TUESDAY, MAY 9, 1995

Friends who hadn't gotten through the night before called to say they'd seen us on *American Journal.* Everyone I spoke to was supportive.

Suddenly Josh and I were being recognized in the grocery store and just about anywhere we went. A lot of women came up to me expressing their heartfelt sympathy for what we were going through, always asking how Josh was doing.

"I don't know what I would do if it was my ex-husband," was the general consensus.

At 9:30 A.M., Director Prillaman called to apologize for the Monday mix-up and to inform me that the trip was rescheduled for the following day, at the same unholy time in the morning. And would I please remember to bring the suitcase with the clothes they had requested.

Next it was my soon-to-be ex-husband Lee on the phone, cursing and carrying on about his family name being bandied about in the papers. I hung up. He called back. I hung up again.

Then it was someone from *PrimeTime* asking if a Kent Devereaux was authorized to represent me.

"Why?" seemed an appropriate question.

Seems during his discussions with the program

regarding deleting some of the footage and digitizing Josh's face, Mr. Devereaux argued that it should never have been filmed in the first place and that the boy's mother was irresponsible for having allowed it.

That was all it took. My nerves were already frazzled. No one was going to refer to me as irresponsible when it came to my son. Devereaux was history as far as I was concerned.

I called Andy, told him what had happened, and that I was going to dismiss Kent Devereaux. He wanted me to think about this decision and not overreact. I gave it a minute, which was about how long it took for me to locate Kent Devereaux's business card, then I dialed his number.

Firing him was one of the toughest things I've ever done. I'm headstrong and impulsive and I know it, but I'd made up my mind.

"Kent," I began. "This is Lana Padilla. Certain things have come to my attention today and I want to tell you they've upset me so much I've decided I don't want you to represent Josh anymore."

He was shocked. He'd probably never been pulled off a case before, especially by someone he was representing for practically nothing.

We talked about the incident, and he tried to gloss over it. He didn't, however, deny that he'd said the things that had been attributed to him. He tried to explain that in the course of playing hardball with the program, he tried to use my naïveté as an excuse. And yes, he may have erred in judgment, but he meant no offense.

Besides, I needed him to represent Josh and he had already set a lot of wheels in motion. He asked that I step back and think about it, not make a decision based on my mood at the moment. He was glib and persuasive, trying to reason with me.

"Calm down and take a few minutes to think about it," he proposed. "Then, if you feel the same way . . ."

"All right," I conceded, "I'll think about it. I'll call you back in five minutes."

He almost had me. He'd almost talked me out of letting him go. I was actually sweating. Suddenly I wasn't sure firing him was the right thing to do. He had, after all, been trying to protect Josh. And he was the expert.

I dialed his number a second time.

"Kent, I haven't changed my mind," I said strongly, despite the fact that my kneecaps were banging into each other underneath the table. "I'm just not going to be comfortable working with you any longer."

He deferred to my decision with dignity, but I knew he was seething.

I hung up, called Andy, and asked him about the other attorney he had tried to get.

"Stan Hunterton," he replied. "I'll call him."

"Hunterton, huh?" I mused. "The FBI also suggested him."

C. Stanley Hunterton was the polar opposite of Kent Devereaux. He was a soft-spoken, round-faced, grandfatherly type. He carried a battered old leather briefcase with straps, and you knew at a glance you could trust him. No flash. Just solid.

And being as straightforward as I am, within five minutes after meeting him, I asked how much he was going to charge us for his services.

"In a case like this, there will be no charge for my services," he said quietly. "This is a national tragedy, and I think as Americans, any of us who can do something to help should do it. Besides, you and Josh are victims, too."

Hunterton stayed for over an hour, taking notes all the time, then said he wanted to get to his office and make some calls.

"As for tomorrow," he said, rising, "I will accompany

you to Oklahoma City for your grand-jury testimony. Of course, you know you're not allowed to have an attorney in the room when you're being questioned.

"However, if you are unsure about anything you're asked, you are permitted to step outside the court and confer with your attorney. I will be in the hallway."

"Can I come, too?" Josh asked.

His request surprised me. "I thought you didn't want to go to Oklahoma," I challenged.

"I just saw on the news that they're transferring my dad there. Maybe they'll let me see him."

I looked at Stan.

"I rather doubt they'll let you visit him at this point," the lawyer replied, "but I suppose there's no harm in you coming."

Josh's face showed a half smile for the first time in weeks.

We were all surprised when 7:30 rolled around and we tuned in *American Journal* only to find that we were again the lead story. They had gotten enough material to spread the segment over two nights, although no one had informed us of this decision.

I cloistered myself in my bedroom for the half hour, busying myself with notes and trying to collect my thoughts about the day. It would have been too much to try to gather thoughts from the week, or even the past forty-eight hours. One day was all I could handle, and I wasn't positive I'd even manage that.

WEDNESDAY, MAY 10, 1995

Not a great morning.

It was bad enough we had to get up at five o'clock again, but there was bad news on the lawn.

On the front page of the *Las Vegas Review-Journal* was the banner headline, FBI QUESTIONS NICHOLS' SON. I was astounded, less by the words than by the fact that there, big as life, was Josh's seventh-grade middle-school yearbook picture side by side with the haunting sketch of John Doe #2. How dare they exploit him like that.

The story quoted the Associated Press as saying there was speculation that federal officials were giving some credence to the possibility that the composite was actually a picture of Terry Nichols's twelve-year-old son. According to a federal official quoted in the article, "He's large for his age—a big kid. Because of his size, it is possible that someone mistook him for an adult. It's a possible explanation."

Only to an idiot, I thought. Josh doesn't have a tattoo, seldom wears baseball caps, and doesn't have a square jaw or a stubbly beard. Then I remembered how Debbie Calhoun had laid out the pictures for me at FBI headquarters, and how she had me reeling and temporarily confused.

There was no question that the story about Josh being questioned and the John Doe theory had been leaked to the press by the government. Certainly neither Josh nor I had said anything.

Normally, at 6:00 A.M. on a Wednesday, there's very little commotion at McCarran International Airport. The weekend tourists have already winged their way back home, and the new batch hasn't yet arrived. From the curb everything appeared quiet, but once we made our way inside, it was a zoo, with reporters and cameramen. We were under siege.

They followed us to the gate area, some of them being courteous enough to snap pictures from a distance, all of them asking if Josh was going to testify. For many of them, it was the first time they had gotten to see Josh in person, which I hoped would put to rest any suspicions about him resembling a thirty-year-old adult.

Josh was also wearing a short-sleeved shirt that made it evident he had no tattoos.

We had a forty-five-minute stopover at Phoenix's Sky Harbor Airport, where we changed planes. Agents Calhoun and MacArthur kept a cautious eye out for enterprising reporters. Fortunately, no one bothered us. After getting coffee, papers, and snacks, we boarded Flight 689 bound for Oklahoma City.

Nothing could have prepared us for the media attack we were subjected to in Oklahoma at Will Rogers World Airport. We were under attack from the moment we stepped out of the jetway. There were lights, cameras, and more reporters than I'd ever seen at one time.

It was a mob scene. You'd think Garth Brooks or the Beatles had landed. People were shouting questions, shoving elongated boom mikes in our faces, and dogging our every step. It was chaos.

Reporters were yelling questions from all angles.

"Do you think Terry did it?"

"Is Josh going to testify?"

"Is Josh John Doe number two?"

"Do you know Tim McVeigh? Does Josh know him?"

"What else was in the storage shed? Why do you think Terry went to the Philippines? Have you talked to Terry since he was arrested?"

"Will you be visiting your ex-husband while you're here?"

And all the time the FBI did little to protect us. There was no excuse for this. They had purposely allowed this degrading episode to happen. The scene was so frenetic it reminded me of people trying to flee a burning building. They swarmed us.

"Do you know how to build a bomb?" someone shouted at Josh. "Did your dad build the bomb? Did you help him?"

This was cruel and unusual punishment.

Why hadn't we been taken off the plane privately, on the tarmac? It would have been easy for them to arrange for a car to come around and pick us up and avoid all of this humiliation.

The FBI was not remotely prepared for the hordes of press. They had made no special arrangements, which was really stupid. Considering what had happened with the media in Vegas, they should have contacted the Oklahoma City bureau and taken steps to avoid the same fiasco.

Even more ridiculous, the FBI agents had to stop at a Budget car-rental location to rent two vehicles. While they answered all the routine questions, Josh, Stan, and I stood a few feet away, completely exposed to the encroaching horde of media people who had formed a circle around us.

"May I see your driver's license? How many days will you be needing the car?" and my favorite, "Where will be you be staying while you're in Oklahoma City?"

Good question. And every reporter within forty miles strained his ears to hear.

To deflect attention away from us, Stan turned and announced who he was, then moved to a different area to give an impromptu press conference, during which he asked for courtesy toward his clients, especially Josh. While he held court, Debbie, Josh, and MacArthur, and I slipped away.

We managed to make it to the Budget lot, get the cars, and motor to a Holiday Inn without being followed. The agents must have taken some extra precautions on their route to the hotel, because by the time we arrived, Stan was already in his room, having taken a taxi from the airport.

The irony of this whole sorry affair is that after all the frenzied activity, we spent two full days in Oklahoma City cooped up in a plain-Jane motel room without me testifying or even meeting anyone from the U.S. attorney's office.

In essence we wasted our time.

Josh spent some time in Stan's room early Wednesday, which allowed the two of them to get better acquainted. This was important because Stan needed to gain Josh's trust. I certainly didn't have it. I was his mother, but he hadn't forgiven me for opening the package Terry had left before his trip to the Philippines.

In his mind, I was probably the major cause of his dad's problems.

Wednesday, May 10, the day we arrived in Oklahoma was also the day Terry was transferred there from Kansas. Some people have speculated that this was the reason why my testifying was put on the back burner. Certainly Terry's transfer drew the attention, but I had a hunch the government had anticipated his coming.

I think they just wanted to play mind games with Terry, and were using Josh as bait. They hoped if Terry saw the media pressure Josh was facing, saw how he was under constant attack from the press about the John Doe #2 situation, Terry might crack.

It all figured. The media crunch in Vegas, the pandemonium in Oklahoma City, and two days of seclusion. I felt lonely, cranky, and had a serious case of the blahs.

Stan went to the Oklahoma prosecutor's office in the afternoon to read the 302s Josh had given in Las Vegas. Josh and I stayed in the hotel, our eyes riveted to the TV, hoping to hear fresh news about Terry.

In the evening, *PrimeTime* and Diane Sawyer had their crack at us. Stung as they were by the fact that *American Journal* had aired the previous two nights, I really thought ABC would delay its segment another week, but they decided to go on the attack, perhaps hoping to ride the wave of *AJ* publicity.

Besides, we were hot news right now.

ABC promoted the piece heavily and ran it in its entirety. And despite my protestations, they blatantly exploited the part where Josh mentioned knowing how to build a bomb. They did, however, make a concession and digitized his face, which by now wasn't necessary since every photographer in America had seen his baby blues.

The TV programs generated tons of publicity, and quotes from the shows had the media buzzing again. I can see now how the shows also sent shock waves through the prosecution and defense teams.

Based on my "on-air" comments, I'll bet they didn't quite know what to make of my position. Would I make a better witness for the prosecution or for the defense? I was sympathetic to Terry, standing fast in my belief that he was not the type of person to have committed any crime that would hurt people, especially children, yet I was the one who opened his personal letter to Tim McVeigh and could verify the seemingly incriminating items he had secreted away in the AAAABCO storage unit.

I purposely watched another program while *PrimeTime* was on. A lot of what I said on the program I didn't remember, and didn't want to. It was like something that had happened in another life.

At 11:30 P.M., I turned off the light and clutched my pillow. I wasn't afraid of the dark. It was a great hiding place, especially when it seems like the whole world is trying to find you.

There had been no word about my testifying before the grand jury. The original plan had been for me to meet with the prosecutor's office on Wednesday afternoon to discuss the general nature of the questions and to go before the jury on Thursday.

I couldn't guess what the new plan would be.

THURSDAY, MAY 11, 1995

We were trapped in the room again, and I felt sorriest for Josh. Stan had told me privately that he held absolutely no hope of seeing his dad.

"The security is too tight and they haven't even set up visiting rules yet," he said.

News reports had said Terry was being held at El Reno Federal Prison, about thirty miles outside Oklahoma City. It was the same place McVeigh was being held, but they were in separate wings, with no other prisoners allowed near them. And they could not talk to each other.

Terry was formally charged in Oklahoma on this day and that news dominated the newscasts.

All of us were anxious to leave. It seemed pretty certain I wouldn't testify on this trip. I was very frustrated that I couldn't do what I had come to do.

Josh was heartbroken that he was in the same town, so close to his dad, yet couldn't see or touch him. I noticed how he moved closer to the TV when pictures of his dad came on the screen.

Late in the afternoon it was decided that we would definitely leave the next morning.

Josh had a nightmare that night, and came crawling into my bed around 3:00 A.M. I wasn't asleep. I had just been lying their, wide-awake, overwhelmed by it all.

FRIDAY, MAY 12, 1995

We awoke at 4:00 A.M. and began to get ready for our *escape*, a word I emphasize because that is what we were doing, in no unceertain terms. We were escorted by a back way into Will Rogers Airport and to a private gate area where our bags were checked and a security officer used a handheld detector to check our luggage and person.

The flight back was much like the flight out. We sat in the very rear of the plane, packed in between the FBI agents. The pilot and flight attendant announced over the intercom that the rear lavatory was out of order, and that passengers should use the front rest room.

There was nothing wrong with the one nearest us, but

the announcement did keep other passengers from approaching us. Josh found a rear row empty and used it to stretch out as best he could. He slept from Oklahoma to Phoenix, where we changed planes for the final leg into McCarran.

During the stopover in Phoenix, we were ushered into a Southwest employee lounge where flight attendants waiting to depart as well as various Arizona counter personnel were relaxing. Some were eating lunch. Newspapers from all sections of the country, probably discarded on earlier flights, were scattered over the chairs and tables.

It was weird. All these stories about us in every paper, and here we were.

At McCarran, we were met by a convoy of three FBI cars, the lead one driven by Director Randy Prillaman. They took us off through the tarmac area, but one especially enterprising press photographer with a long-range lens got a shot of us anyway.

Prillaman and Agent Gough transported us home, and I soon found out why we were getting the special treatment.

"I'd like you to give me whatever hats or baseball caps Josh owns," said Prillaman when we got to our front door. "And if you don't mind, I'd like Agents Calhoun and MacArthur to take another quick walk through the house."

They took six of Josh's baseball caps, some of which he hadn't worn in years. Why they did so was no secret. They wanted to see if any of them resembled the cap John Doe #2 was wearing in the sketch.

I knew they were flogging a dead horse, but they just wouldn't abandon their theory.

"I suppose we'll be hearing in the next day or two when they'll want you to return to Oklahoma," Prillaman said just before leaving.

"I can hardly wait," I said sarcastically.

Minutes later I was in my bed, weeping buckets of bitter tears into a pillow I held on to for dear life.

Never before in my life had I gone to sleep at 11:00 A.M.

And I slept until the next day.

7

WHY?

It was the single-most-asked question in America.

Why the bombing?

Why Oklahoma City?

On the surface, the why of the bombing seemed fairly simple. It was a terrorist attack by right-wing antigovernment dissidents gone haywire.

There were dozens of theories as to the why of Oklahoma City, and I heard many of them, thanks to reporters, well-meaning friends, anonymous callers, and private investigators all eager to tell me what they heard and add their own spin to the situation. And more for Josh's sake than anything else, I listened, and tried to weigh the likelihood that there were possible suspects other than Terry and Tim.

Revenge for Waco, for the government's "reckless disregard" for the Branch Davidians and their children was the most prevalent theory. Others contended that Oklahoma was merely a line in the sand. That the bombing was a violent warning to a government that had become too big and too overbearing.

Some claimed that the destruction of the Murrah Federal Building was actually the work of foreign terrorists and that Tim McVeigh was a low-level peon in their pay.

This idea was even supported by some federal officials in Washington, where investigators begging anonymity told reporters that they suspected McVeigh was merely a "foot soldier" in the plot.

But the most intriguing, and maybe the most bizarre, theory was proposed by militia groups who claimed the U.S. government itself had actually blown up the building in an attempt to disrupt a planned commemorative vigil by sympathizers in Waco and to turn the country against the rising swell of paramilitary groups.

Rumors spread that Bureau of Alcohol, Tobacco and Firearms and federal agents in the building had advance warning of the bombing and that many of them had called in sick on April 19,1995.

If the FBI and ATF were brazen enough to murder women and children at the Branch Davidian complex, then have a government panel absolve them of any responsibility, why not blow up a federal building as well? one radio show asked.

It would have been easier to swallow if the terrorists had been Middle Eastern, or of any other foreign nationality. After all, terrorism was their game, their way of life. They were fanatics. America could have accepted this act of insanity from outsiders. But as the smoke cleared and the body count mounted, a cold, sobering reality shocked us all to our roots.

The threat was not just *to* the heartland of America, it was *from* and *by* the heartland of America. We had met the enemy and it was us. America had shot itself in the foot.

One Richard Wayne Snell provided an interesting footnote to the frenzy of speculation, even if he wasn't a piece of the puzzle. A convicted double murderer, Snell was executed in Arkansas on the same day as the Murrah Federal Building bombing took place.

The oddity of this is that Snell, an Oklahoman, had

been implicated in a plot to blow up the same structure twelve years earlier, according to information gathered by a federal prosecutor.

The plot was concocted by a group of white supremacists with neo-Nazi ties in October of 1983. It called for parking a van or trailer in front of the federal building and blowing it up with rockets triggered by a timer. Although there are no apparent links between Snell and the April 19,1995, bombing or either of the suspects charged, Snell's execution had been protested by right-wing paramilitary groups who labeled him a patriot and called the federal government "the Beast."

Details of the 1983 plot came from James D. Ellison, founder of a now defunct anti-Semitic paramilitary group called the Covenant, the Sword and the Arm of the Lord. Ellison told Federal Prosecutor Steven N. Snyder that the leaders behind the 1983 plot discussed how to topple the government using a book called *The Turner Diaries* as a guideline. Ellison also told the prosecutor that at Snell's request he had checked out the federal building in Oklahoma City to gauge what it would take to level or destroy it.

I guess there was just something about the building that made it a target. Maybe it was the Mount Everest of Federal Buildings. Extremists wanted to blow it up just because it was there.

A newspaper report claimed that Snell spent the final hours before his execution watching television coverage of the Oklahoma City bombing. An observer said he was appalled by what he saw. Nevertheless, his last words, directed at Arkansas governor Jim Guy Tucker, were anything but sorrowful. "Governor Tucker, look over your shoulder," he intoned. "Justice is coming. I wouldn't trade places with you or any of your cronies. Hell has victories. I am at peace."

Acquaintances said Snell was bitter toward the

government because of the IRS. Agents from the Oklahoma city office had reportedly taken him to court and then seized his property. Hearing this, I wondered how much of the hatred Snell felt and *The Turner Diaries* advocated had seeped into the consciousnesses of the murderers who had destroyed the Alfred P. Murrah Federal Building on April 19,1995.

One thing that bothered me from the outset and still confuses me today was a live radio report that claimed Tim McVeigh and a companion, possibly of *Middle Eastern* descent, were seen in the vicinity of the Murrah Building minutes before it exploded. The report, broadcast in the first hours after the blast, was confirmed by police sources in Oklahoma, then never mentioned again.

What happened to the man who could have been John Doe #2? This has never been explained to my satisfaction and it casts a giant shadow over my own efforts to solve the mystery of the Oklahoma bombing.

The Turner Diaries, by the way, a novel published in 1978 by William Pierce, a reclusive ultraconservative white supremacist who wrote under the name of Andrew MacDonald, was a clear call to arms against the federal govenment. More interestingly, it appears to be a step-by-step blueprint for the Oklahoma City bombing. According to Jerry Dale, a former sheriff of Hillsboro, West Virginia, where novelist Pierce now resides, *The Turner Diaries* is a manual for terrorism, and it will chill you to the bone."

In the novel, white supremacists and anti-Semitic forces destroy a federal building and kill hundreds of people, using a bomb made from fertilizer and heating oil. The bomb explodes at 9:15 A.M. The devastation is so great that it takes more than two weeks to recover the bodies of the deceased.

The Murrah Building explosion happened at 9:04 A.M.

and the device was a homemade bomb made of ammonium nitrate, fertilizer, and hatred. It took nearly three weeks to recover the bodies of the workers and the children in the day-care center who had been killed in the blast.

The resemblance between fiction and reality was so frightening that it sent me scurrying to the library to try to find out more about the *Diaries*. When I read it, one particular section gave me the willies, and I quote it here:

> As carefully as we could we calculated that we should have at least 10,000 pounds of TNT or an equivalent explosive to destroy a substantial portion of the building and wreck the new computer center in the sub-basement. To be on the safe side, we asked for 20,000 pounds.
>
> Instead what we have is a little under 5,000 pounds of ammonium nitrate fertilizer, which is much less effective than TNT for our purpose. . . .
>
> Sensitized with oil and tightly confined, it makes an effective blasting agent where the aim is simply to move a quantity of dirt and rock. But our original plan for the bomb called for it to be essentially unconfined and to be able to punch through two levels of re-inforced concrete flooring while producing an open air blast wave powerful enough to blow the facade off a massive and strongly constructed building.

There were reports that Tim McVeigh had read *The Turner Diaries*. Investigators had asked me if I had ever heard of the book, or if I knew whether or not Terry had read it. I hadn't heard of it at the time and had no idea if he'd read it.

But I did know that McVeigh had long expressed antigovernment views, had written letters to newspapers protesting actions of the government, and had become disillusioned with the army when he failed to qualify for Special Forces. He had also insisted that the government had surgically inserted a computer chip in his buttocks, a theory steadfastly supported by a number of far-right radicals and ex-military personnel. I had even read that Tim McVeigh's driver's license had been issued on April 19, 1993, the exact day of the invasion and terror at the Branch Davidian complex. No sane person could believe those dates were a mere coincidence.

But why Oklahoma City?

Because it was in the center of the country? Because it probably had looser security than facilities in a major city such as Los Angeles, Dallas, or Washington? This made sense, but a reference I saw buried in a long article in the *Dallas Morning News* struck me as being the most plausible explanation.

Although federal officials had downplayed the idea that the bomb was aimed at any one person or organization, the name Bob Ricks may as well have been in lights on a Las Vegas marquee.

Ricks was the FBI's chief spokesman during the fifty-one-day siege of—you guessed it—the Branch Davidian compound in Waco. And he was the special agent in charge of the bureau's Oklahoma City headquarters.

How about Ricks being the number-one reason Oklahoma City was the target?

Oklahoma City is also the state headquarters for the Federal Bureau of Alcohol, Tobacco and Firearms, and agents from the Oklahoma field office played a key role in the Waco massacre.

You didn't need Sherlock Holmes to put these pieces together.

However, McVeigh, or whoever actually planned and

carried out the bombing, missed one very important point: Agent Ricks did not work out of the Murrah Building. His office was located in another building some two miles from the downtown federal offices.

Whenever television specials focused on the case, and offered theories about why it happened, Josh and I listened for the name Bob Ricks. We never heard it.

During one program, on which Attorney General Janet Reno reiterated her call for the death penalty for the perpetrators, Josh came rushing out of his room, upset and agitated. "Does this mean they're going to give my dad the death penalty?" he asked. "Even if Tim did it alone?" (So far, Terry had not been charged in the bombing and was basically being held as a material witness, although all the lawyers and federal officials I spoke to indicated that it was just a matter of time until he was indicted.)

Josh's chin was quivering and he was fighting back the tears that were sure to come if I told him what I really believed. In my heart I knew that once Terry was charged, the government would attempt to have him and McVeigh tried together so they could paint them both with the same shade of guilt. If one got the death penalty, both would.

It was unfair, but that's the way the system worked. It had been explained to me that in a case where there are two defendants, the ideal game plan for the prosecution is to have them tried together. That way one cannot put blame on the other in the hope of getting a lighter sentence. For just that reason, however, the defense would push for separate trials. It was to the defense's advantage to have each of the defendants blaming the other and playing on the sympathy of their respective juries.

In answer to Josh's question, I had to admit that I didn't know. "We'll just have to wait and see," I said.

"I'm sure your dad's lawyers are going to do everything they can. He has one of the best lawyers in the country."

The answer wasn't convincing enough.

Josh whirled and went back into his room, slamming the door and collapsing heavily onto his bed. He turned the stereo in his room to an ear-piercing level to drown out his sobs. But I hurt anyway. I knew he was crying. Crying for a father he might never get to spend time growing up with, ever again.

8

IT'S REALLY A MIRACLE ANY OF US SURVIVED MAY.

I don't think I ever caught my breath, got a full night's sleep, or relaxed. When I did sleep, I had nightmares.

Josh and Terry probably summarized it best.

"With all that went on, I thought April was two months long," Terry told Josh during one of his weekly phone calls.

"I don't remember May at all either," Josh confided as he came out on the patio to tell me about his dad's call. "I guess I just blanked it out. So many things happened every day, I never knew what day it was."

I could vouch for that. Josh had no idea the number of nights I lay awake, listening to him bang around the house because he couldn't sleep. Sometimes I would come out to check on him. Just to try to talk to him, but he usually didn't want company.

One especially memorable night I awoke to find him hunched over the dining-room table, intently studying a road atlas. He had one of his old school rulers in his hand and he was painstakingly measuring things on the small colored pages.

"What are you doing?" I asked.

"Measuring how far it is from Junction City, Kansas, to Oklahoma City," he said without looking up.

He had heard reports of his dad driving from destination to destination within a certain time period and he was doing his own calculations to see if the accusations had merit. That's how interested he was in helping his father.

"It's too many miles," he said finally. "My dad couldn't have done it because he wouldn't have had time."

Other nights I'd find him staring silently at the muted TV, transfixed by the light-and-dark images as they danced across the screen. One salvation for him was his music. I didn't always agree with his choices, especially the rap stuff, but it did keep him occupied and seemed to take his mind off his problems.

He fell into the habit of putting on his earphones and lying in bed, often falling asleep with them pressed against his head. In the morning I'd gently remove them, but by then he was sleeping so soundly a thunderclap wouldn't have roused him.

I suppose it was just as well that he stayed up until he was so exhausted that he had no choice but to sleep, because when he did sleep, he'd have bad dreams. He'd tell me he dreamed about the guards beating his dad, or starving him. He wondered if Terry was getting enough exercise and if they were giving him things to read. The kind of things most twelve-year-olds wouldn't think about.

Josh couldn't seem to get enough information about his dad. He didn't read the papers but he watched CNN religiously, and when he saw articles about Terry he insisted I read them to him.

When something didn't seem right to him, he questioned it. There were times he wanted to call the FBI, or Stan, to get a clarification.

It reminded me of one of the nights we were in custody. Josh had gone through some intensive questioning earlier in the day and seemed pretty tired when we returned to the hotel. He climbed into bed about 10:30 and seemed to be sound asleep by eleven.

I was reading when he awoke screaming, "I want to talk to Debbie. Right now. I've got something important to tell her."

I knew he meant Debbie Calhoun, the agent who had been interrogating him. If he wanted to talk to her at 11:30 P.M., it must be something crucial to the case. My first reaction was to worry.

Maybe he'd thought of some key evidence, or remembered a picture she'd shown him. Maybe he had information that would lead the agents to the real bombers. I really didn't want to ask him because I didn't want to know.

"Are you sure it can't wait until tomorrow?" I asked.

"I'm positive," he insisted. "Please get her on the phone. Call the FBI. They'll give you her home number."

I knew the FBI's number by heart, but they wouldn't give out Agent Calhoun's home number. They did, however, patch us through to her at home. When she answered, I said, "Debbie? It's Lana Padilla. I'm sorry to bother you so late, but Josh insisted he had to talk to you and it couldn't wait until morning."

"That's okay," she said sleepily.

I handed Josh the phone. Since there was really no place for me to go, I was about to hear whatever he had to tell her whether I wanted to or not.

"Debbie, it's Josh. I just wanted to say, since I helped you out today, I want you to help my dad."

Funny. It was a childlike request, yet he was negotiating like an adult. He figured he'd given the FBI some type of informational help and he wanted compensation in the form of leniency for his dad. He really was a remarkable kid.

When he hung up, I just sort of stared at him and he looked back as if to ask, "What are you looking at?"

"What?" he finally said.

"I was just thinking about how much you love your dad," I said. "I wish you loved me that much."

"Aw, Mom," he said, putting his arm around me. "I love you."

"What was that all about?" I asked, my curiosity getting the better of me.

"They asked me if I knew any of Tim's friends. They wanted to know who we saw or talked to when Dad and I went to Kingman.

"Debbie wanted to know if I could think of anyone who might know the type of person Tim was. I told them to go and talk to Michael Fortier. He was Tim's friend. He was in the army with Dad and Tim at Fort Riley."

Over the next two days the name Michael Fortier became a household word. CNN showed footage of the FBI taking him out of his Kingman trailer home in handcuffs. He was definitely a key player in the case, and Josh had given them the lead.

Now he was asking for what he considered a reasonable payback. Go easy on his dad.

Somehow we had muddled through the first two weeks of the month. The flight that the FBI canceled at the airport; the futile three-day trip when Josh, Stan, and I flew to Oklahoma City without my testifying; the haggling, then the airing of *PrimeTime*, the two segments of *American Journal,* and all the attendant publicity.

But now the dress rehearsals were over.

The word came down, from the FBI to Stan, that my appearance before the grand jury had been rescheduled. I was due to appear May 18. We would travel on the morning of the seventeenth.

I was skeptical. No matter what they said, I wasn't sure it was going to happen. Been there, haven't done that, I thought.

And contrary to my nature, when inquiring press minds called to ask if I knew when I was going back to Oklahoma, I actually pleaded ignorance.

"I'm waiting to hear," I lied. "I guess they don't need me yet."

At times it was tough to be evasive because I knew the media people were just doing their jobs, and what harm could it do for me to help them out? Through all the questioning, I did learn that some of the media people were better at their jobs than others. And Josh and I did develop a special relationship with a couple of sincere reporters who honored my requests to keep certain things off the record or to hold a story until a more opportune time.

I think my two favorites were Pete Slover of the *Dallas Morning News* and Bob Vito of CNN. They were always fair, and more important, always accurate with quotes, and both seemed to have Josh and my best interest at heart. In addition, even though they had to push for stories like everyone else, they showed us respect and on more than one occasion demonstrated that they realized we were just ordinary people caught up in extraordinary circumstances.

MAY 17, 1995

This was the day. I could feel in my bones that there would be no more delays or problems. The grand jury was finally going to get its chance at Terry Nichols's ex-wife.

The FBI and Stan were all concerned about my safety, but I don't think I was ever really afraid. I went along with their precautions just to humor them, because I couldn't believe anyone would want to kill me. For what? Throughout this whole ordeal, I had always been more worried about someone trying to hurt Josh or something happening to Terry while he was in jail.

Josh wasn't going to Oklahoma this time. Just Stan, me, and FBI agent Dick MacArthur.

My doorbell rang just before 6:00 A.M. and I was

surprised to find myself face-to-face with an agent I'd never seen before. He said good morning, showed me his identification, and I opened the door. Stan had not yet made an appearance.

"I'll only be driving you to the airport," he said, more to make conversation than to ease my mind. "Agent MacArthur will meet us there."

When Stan arrived, we piled our bags into the agent's car, I left a note for Josh and an emergency twenty dollars I knew he'd find reason to spend, and we were off.

McCarran was only six or seven minutes from my house via the new airport connector, and at six in the morning we had the road to ourselves. There were no signs of media people, but it wouldn't have mattered if they had been out in droves. The agent cruised past the normal parking garages to a special secluded area, then around a back entrance, up some stairs, and into the Metro Police office in the airport.

Dick MacArthur was waiting for us.

I found the continued absence of the press curiously calming. I had certainly had enough of the cameras. And the questions.

We didn't board with the regular passengers. Arrangements had been made for us to join the Southwest flight from the tarmac. We all knew the flight route. Las Vegas to Phoenix, a forty-five-minute stopover, change planes, then two hours nonstop to Oklahoma City. And no real food. Sodas, honey-roasted peanuts, and a crowded plane.

An Arizona-based FBI agent met us in Phoenix and chatted with Dick MacArthur during the stopover. I think he was there just to offer backup and to keep us from being hassled. No one recognized me, or if they did, they decided to keep their distance.

I read for a few minutes, then slept the remainder of the way to Oklahoma City.

Agent Barry White met us in Oklahoma. Another time, another place I would have been flippant and told him I liked his sexy music, but instead I offered an obligatory smile and let MacArthur and Stan listen to his game plan.

We were out of Will Rogers Airport and into Agent White's waiting car in a very short time, and as I sat in the backseat I wondered again about the FBI. They really were calling the shots. When they wanted us in and out in a hurry, they arranged it, and when they wanted us to be inconvenienced, exposed, or harassed, they could manage it simply by doing nothing. They could use us and abuse us as they wished.

"That's where you'll be staying," Agent White said as we drove by a sunbaked Best Western. "The U.S. attorney's office wanted you to come downtown first so they could interview you and get that out of the way."

I felt my stomach growl and I wasn't sure if I was hungry or merely having anxiety pains. At the U.S. attorney's office, Agent White called upstairs and was advised that things were running a little behind schedule and that it would be at least forty-five minutes before we were needed.

A little restaurant on the building's ground floor looked inviting, so Stan, MacArthur, and I stepped in for lunch. Agent White excused himself, saying we could go directly to the fourth-floor offices when we finished lunch.

Stan and I ordered Caesar salads while Agent MacArthur opted for a turkey sandwich on white. I headed for a phone to call home while our orders were being prepared.

After we ate, MacArthur went for a walk while Stan talked to me about what was going to happen. His coaching was calm, and he explained each step we would go through, both upstairs and at the grand jury. He had been a U.S. prosecutor in Detroit, so he was very familiar with the procedures. He was a good teacher and I felt prepared.

We took the elevator to the fourth floor, then walked through an upright metal detector at the entrance to the U.S. attorney's office. The security guards appeared to have no interest in who we were and continued talking about the new security detectors that had been ordered as an additional safeguard against terrorism.

Stan held open the left side of the double glass doors and approached the receptionist. "They're still not quite ready for us," he reported. "Let's have a seat for a minute." Like most government offices, the lobby was more functional than comfortable.

I picked up a magazine and flipped through it without seeing any of the articles. When something moved outside the glass doors, it caught my eye; even though I couldn't see clearly through the frosted glass I thought I recognized the forms.

"I think that's Marife and Nicole out there," I said to Stan, nodding toward the doorway. I got up, opened the door, and sure enough, there were Marife and Nicole. We were surprised to see each other.

Marife and I hugged, holding each other tightly, as if we were each grasping a life preserver. Nicole was wide-eyed, her little brown ponytail bobbing as she eyed me suspiciously. She did not recognize me until I announced, "Hi, Nicole. I'm Josh's mother."

"'Osh," she said excitedly. "'Osh," And she looked around for Josh.

It was a touching and poignant moment. Terry Nichols's current wife and ex-wife locked in an emotional embrace, tears streaming down both their puzzled faces. Marife was there to be questioned just as I was, and she quickly told me she and Nicole had been in custody for a month, unable to go home, living in hotels, having little or no contact with the outside world.

She was so young. I felt no jealousy toward her. In fact, I thought of her more as a daughter than as a woman who had married my ex-husband. I know I certainly thought of adorable little Nicole as a granddaughter. I had respect for her because Josh's father was her husband. Both Nicole and Marife loved Josh, and throughout the months of this case Marife has called Josh regularly, just to talk, and see how he is.

"Have you seen Terry?" I asked.

"No. Not yet, and I don't know if they're going to let me see him," she replied.

I must have asked five thousand questions in the five minutes we were together. Neither of us wanted our time together to end. There was so much to say. So many questions.

As I said, she looked so young, even younger than her twenty-three years. And here she was being thrust into a crisis situation in an unfamiliar country. How could she possibly cope? She didn't know her rights. Who was going to protect her?

I was sure it was easy for the FBI and other authorities to get her to do or say whatever they wanted. How would she know not to? The fact that she was held for thirty-four days without a lawyer was indication enough. She had not been permitted to talk to Terry during all that time and the government had been allowed to interrogate her at will.

Our conversation was over too soon. A young attorney came through and escorted Marife and Nicole into another office, and as I watched her walk away I thought about how she had come into Terry's life, and some of the struggles they had endured in the short five years they had known each other. None of it had been smooth for them. Their lives had been marked by tragedy and hardship ever since Terry's first visit to the Philippines in late November of 1989.

It was clear to me now that Terry had made the trip to Cebu city with the express intention of finding a Filipino bride. His Philippine vacation was arranged by a company called Paradise Shelton Tours, a bride service based in Scottsdale, Arizona. "When he got here, he told me he wanted to meet girls," said Daisy Legaspi, a guide at an illegal bride service in Cebu. "Mr. Nichols told me he had many friends who had Filipino wives and they were very happy."

However, the Cebu foreign tourists see and the one Marife Torres grew up in are worlds apart. Tourists see the city's inviting beaches, its international airport, and the beautiful women on the travel brochures. Marife Torres, the third of six children, had just graduated from high school, but instead of seeing a bright future, she saw streets lined with garbage and a dead-end life unless she found a way out of the tiny shack where her family resided.

Terry Nichols, a lonely American in search of a wife, was that way out.

Some reports say Marife was anxious to meet an American, any American who could remove her from her life of poverty. Others say she only met Terry at the insistence of her father, Eduardo Torres, a poorly paid Cebu traffic policeman who wanted to see his daughter make a better life for herself.

Legaspi arranged for Vilma Elumbaring, the Torres's next-door neighbor, to have dinner with Terry.

Elumbaring recalls Terry focusing on three things during their dinner. "He talked about his divorce, his time in the army, and finding a Filipino wife," she said. "The one thing that came across loud and clear was that he was upset over his divorce."

But the fact was, we weren't officially divorced yet. It was all over and done with on paper, but the final dissolution wouldn't happen for another month.

Terry spent the next three weeks in Cebu, swimming at local beaches, shopping for souvenirs, and meeting with potential Filipino business partners, according to published reports. He also told me he spent a lot of time seeing seventeen-year-old Marife Torres. When he returned to Las Vegas to pick up Josh, he told me of his intentions to marry Marife, and that it was important that the divorce be finalized as scheduled, on December 18.

Over the next few months Terry and Marife wrote gushing letters to each other, and in mid-1990 Terry formally proposed. The next time he went to the Philippines, in November 1990, it was to make Marife his bride. They were married on November 20, in a small restaurant in Cebu.

Shortly after the wedding Terry came back to the United States to get settled. Marife had signed a power of attorney and Terry listed her as co-owner of the farmhouse at 4321 Argyle Road in Snover, Michigan. They had arranged for Marife to join him in the States as soon as her U.S. visa was approved. Terry figured it would take a month, give or take a week.

Neither of them expected it to take more than four months. The first of their problems was the delay in getting Marife into the United States. The second was more troublesome.

When he left for the United States, Terry gave Marife a lump sum of money, enough for her to live comfortably until she could join him. But somehow, the newly married Mrs. Nichols didn't manage to live up to her vows. According to her mother, Fey Torres, and her father, Eduardo, Marife went off on a "last fling" with a Filipino boyfriend. A few weeks later she learned she was pregnant by the boyfriend.

It was a trying time for Terry. It was difficult for him to admit the circumstances to anyone, but he talked to me. I felt for him. He was hurt before his marriage had even started. He had gone from a more domineering older woman to a young, and apparently flighty, teenager.

"Follow your heart," I told him. "If you love her, you'll

have to forgive her. If you can't do that, call it off before it goes any further."

I know he did a lot of soul-searching, and it was tough for him because he wanted his own kids. I don't think he was thrilled about the prospect of raising someone else's. Not after Barry and Troy.

Eventually he forgave Marife, and convinced her that he could love the baby as his own. Jason Torres Nichols was born in Henderson, Nevada, just outside Las Vegas, on September 21,1991.

But life in America in general, and Michigan in particular, did not live up to Marife's dream. She became disillusioned quickly and wrote to her parents complaining that she felt like a maid with three husbands. She was cooking, cleaning and tending to James Nichols, Terry, and occasionally Tim McVeigh. It was more than she wanted to handle.

"Marife was angry with Tim because he would come and stay at their house for three or four weeks at a time and expect her to wait on him," said her father in an interview with the *Dallas Morning News*. "She knew Tim was trying to get Terry in the gun business and she saw Tim as a bad person."

And even though Terry couldn't seem to hold a decent job for very long, he did demonstrate that he cared deeply for his wife, and that despite the shaky start of their marriage, he truly loved her.

So much so that he agreed to move to the Philippines in early 1993.

He told me he had made this decision because it would enable him to be closer to Marife while she pursued her education as a physical therapist. Terry had encouraged her in her career, telling her it would be easy to get a job when she had enough schooling.

As it turned out, though, the return to Cebu was a bad idea.

The noise and smog of the city affected Terry's health, he found the heat unbearable, and he became violently ill from some sort of intestinal flu. He spent weeks in bed with diarrhea.

Terry's island paradise had quickly become a tropical purgatory. Less than a month after their great exodus from America, Terry, Marife, and Jason returned to the States, settling in Las Vegas. They were aware that Marife was pregnant with their first child, Nicole.

But Terry didn't stay in Vegas long. After just two and a half months he packed up his family and belongings and headed back to Michigan.

Nicole was born on August 1, 1993.

After enduring the hardship of getting Marife into the country, dealing with her infidelity and pregnancy, their own moves from Michigan to Las Vegas to the Philippines and back again, another tragedy slapped the Nichols family, this one more heart-wrenching than all the others combined.

On November 22, 1993, twenty-six-month-old Jason Torres was found dead in the Nichols home, an apparent victim of accidental suffocation. The boy had somehow gotten his head stuck in a plastic bag while the family slept. Terry and Marife had been preparing to move to Las Vegas for the second time and the bag was part of their packing materials.

Marife was beside herself with grief. She could not understand how such a thing could have happened. She asked authorities to take fingerprints, but they were unable to find any evidence of foul play. Marife and her family were convinced that Jason's death was not an accident.

I remember her calling me, shyly hinting that she wanted my opinion about the possibility that Terry could have been involved in Jason's death.

When she was confident that I could be trusted and would not be insulted by her inquiry, she asked, "Do you think Terry could have done something like this?" She was sobbing as she spoke and a minute later she was gulping for breath as she cried. "Is he capable of doing something this bad?"

"Definitely not," I assured her. "Terry is a good man. He would never do anything to harm a child. There must be some other explanation. Was anyone else around?"

"Only Tim," she said. "Terry's friend, Tim McVeigh."

I didn't tell her what I was thinking when I heard those words.

Marife had had a hard life with Terry thus far, and now was involved in another tragic happening beyond her control.

All of these thoughts flooded my mind that day in Oklahoma City as I watched her walk away, her precious eighteen-month-old Nicole trailing a few steps behind, completely oblivious to where she was or how much trouble her daddy was in.

As if she didn't have enough complications in her life already, Marife was carrying another baby. While in FBI custody, she had discovered that she was pregnant. Terry didn't know yet.

Almost simultaneous with Marife's departure, U.S. Attorney Patrick Ryan entered the office. He said hello to Stan, then to Dick MacArthur, and finally extended his hand to me. He was only passing through, he said, then told us Prosecutor Arlene Joplin would be with us very soon.

She swept into the office about ten minutes later, surrounded by an entourage of assistants.

Her first business was to address Stan and Dick about the logistics of our interview. "I have one more interview to do before I'll be able to get with you," she said, speaking directly to me. "I'm sorry, but something's come up that I can't delay. It would be best if you could come back around five-thirty, if that's not too inconvenient."

Arlene was very good at her job. When we reconvened a little before 5:30, she was both apologetic and friendly. We located a suitable meeting room and got right down to business.

A long conference table was the main piece of furniture in the room. I sat first, electing to sit facing the door. Stan sat to my right, and a female U.S. attorney to my left. Lined up on the other side of the table were Dick MacArthur, Arlene, and an Oklahoma FBI agent. On the table were six or seven files and stacks of phone logs.

Arlene Joplin made it very easy. She just asked leading questions and allowed me to talk.

I was surprised that the questions weren't phrased in a way to trap or coerce me into saying incriminating things about Terry. Most of her inquiries were really designed to establish general information. For example: "I've read that you and Terry had rental property when you were married. Is that correct?" And: "You also invested in gold and silver and penny stocks?"

She was looking to establish an overview, trying to uncover just who Terry Lynn Nichols was and what kind of life he had led. It was also obvious, from later questions regarding the $20,000 I had found in my kitchen and the profits from properties sold when our marriage dissolved, that she wanted to get a line on Terry's personal finances. She wanted to have some direction when she asked questions in front of the grand jury.

A lot of ground was covered in four hours, and when we said goodbye at 9:30, I was tired and hungry.

It was just before 10:00 P.M. when Dick MacArthur wheeled the rental car into the drive-through lane at a Burger King. Stan and I had Whoppers and fries to go.

What a life.

We were told to be ready by 8:15 A.M., but we hadn't been told where we were going; the location of the grand-jury hearings was highly classified.

I was up early. I had breakfast in the hotel coffee shop, alone, busying myself with the morning newspapers. I was nervous and had cramps, not a wonderful combination.

A waitress recognized me from one of the television shows. "Aren't you that lady with the twelve-year-old son and the bombing?" she said disjointedly.

"Shhh," I said, putting a finger to my lips. A look of understanding passed between us and she refilled my cup and moved on.

Stan joined me and eased into the task at hand. He went over some of the questions that he anticipated would be asked. He took nothing for granted.

"I'm going to be right outside the door of the hearing," he reminded me. "Don't worry."

Agent White presented himself a couple minutes later and we loaded into another car and followed him to Tinker Air Force Base, the site of the hearings. It was a gray, windy day with heavy clouds and a threat of rain. A perfect day for something like this. It didn't help my mood.

"We're supposed to be there by nine," White said, even though he hadn't been asked.

At Tinker, we were directed into a small office down the corridor from the hearing room. We had been sitting patiently for about fifteen minutes when a female attorney knocked and came in carrying some papers.

"These are reimbursement forms so you can recover any money you spend on food," she explained. "The government allows you a certain per diem expense." Stan reached for the papers, and as he tucked them in his briefcase I chuckled, wondering if we'd have to present a receipt from the Burger King.

Fifteen minutes later the panel was ready for me.

I walked straight up the center aisle to a table with a microphone in the middle of the room. A chair was situated so I could face the room. Tables for attorneys were to my right, Arlene and her aides were at another table to my left, and the grand-jury panelists were at tables where visitors would have been seated had it been a regular courtroom.

I was sworn in, giving my full name and promising to tell the truth. The whole truth and nothing but.

If my life depended on it, I couldn't recall the first question. I was still in a state of shocked disbelief that all of this was happening. But somehow your body and mind just go through it. They just react instinctively.

I think the first thing I noticed were the panelists, and how they appeared to be everyday people. They weren't in suits and ties. They didn't look like rich people or diplomats. They were moms, dads, grandmas, and grandpas. Regular Joes. That could be me sitting out there, I thought. *But I'm up here. I'm on trial.*

Then Arlene was in front of me, questioning me about the letters. Those damn letters. "For the record I'd like you to read Exhibit A and Exhibit B, Mrs. Padilla," she said.

Those were the letters.

"And please tell us how those letters came into your possession. Were they written to you?"

She wanted me to read the one addressed to me first. It was the one with the words "Read and Do Immediately" printed in bold at the top of the page.

I made it through about four lines before breaking down. It was too painful. I kept thinking, This is Josh's father we're talking about. Not some stranger. It's not like I witnessed a crime committed by some stranger and was being asked to testify and put him away.

Here, everything I said could be turned against

Terry. It could mean life or death for him. They had been talking about the death penalty almost from the beginning, and although it hadn't been formally decided, there was every indication the government was going to press for it.

Arlene handed me a tissue, then asked if I needed some time to compose myself. She pointed to a small door to my rear and instructed the panel that we were going to adjourn for a few minutes.

Outside, I told Stan there was no way I could read the letters. He must have relayed the message to Arlene, because when I returned to the room, she read the letters into evidence.

The questioning droned on, with few, if any, surprises. We covered the gold and silver, our rental properties again, the time line of Josh's visit, touched on Terry's travels to the Philippines, Terry's assets, and how he could possibly have amassed the $20,000 he had stashed behind my kitchen-utensil drawer.

Someone asked how I could have thought he was poverty-stricken when he had all that cash, and I explained that Terry was very conservative about money and very frugal.

I was asked to leave the room for a few minutes, and when I returned, there were a number of questions about Terry's hair color.

"Did he ever dye his hair?" one man asked.

"Not to my knowledge," I replied.

"What is his natural color?" another called out.

I looked around the room, trying to find someone with similar hair.

Finally I spotted a man over to my right. I pointed at him. "Like that," I said loudly, happy I'd found a match. "That's the color of Terry's hair."

Later I learned the hair-color questions were important in determining if Terry had been involved in various robberies. Reportedly, the thief had a distinctive hair color and my comments helped vindicate Terry.

My testimony ran for two and a half hours, from 9:30 until noon. When it was over, I was drained. I said a silent prayer, thanking God it was over.

We had our luggage in the car and seemed to be in good shape to make the 1:30 flight home. It was Southwest's last connecting flight west of the day. We made the airport with minutes to spare and were ushered into a secured area where a security cop with a handheld detector brushed it up and down our bodies.

Finally, I thought, we were done with Oklahoma, but once again I was being naive. I was nowhere near done with the place. My son's father was in prison there. If he wanted to visit, we'd have to come back .

There was going to be a trial, and there was a 90 percent chance I'd have to testify. And it would be in Oklahoma. Arlene Joplin had told me I was an articulate and credible witness when I had finished with the grand jury. "You'll make a solid witness at the trial," she'd said. It was a compliment I'd rather not have gotten.

A Southwest gate agent came by to inform us that the inbound flight had been delayed and it was going to affect our flight. If we couldn't leave on time, we wouldn't be able to make our connection in Phoenix.

It appeared that we would have to stay overnight. They'd have a better idea in half an hour. We sat there with long looks. Stan decided to go browse in the various airport gift shops.

While he was gone an attendant hurried in to tell us that another flight was available. If we hurried, we could board it and make the Phoenix connection. We had to locate Stan, which we did without a moment to spare.

We hustled aboard the alternate flight, cruised into Phoenix and on to Las Vegas, arriving around 6:30 in the evening. We were pleased to be able to deplane without having to fight the press.

That was the good news. The bad news was that they were waiting on my lawn. I rushed directly into the house while Stan remained outside to make a statement. I was crabby and agitated.

Eight hours earlier I was at the center of the most newsworthy event in America. Now I was home to kids, groceries, cleaning house, and doing laundry.

I was famished and I wanted to sleep.

But before I did so, I got to hear a very scary bedtime story, as told by Troy. "While you were gone Barry flipped out and had one of his wild, anything-goes parties," he related.

I looked around. There was no evidence of the party. Barry had covered his tracks fairly well, so I was willing to write it off. No harm, no foul.

"The party wasn't the bad news," Troy continued, and my heart dropped. Barry wasn't home. What could have happened? Had he been arrested?

"I wasn't here at the time, but Josh was. And when things started getting out of control, Josh asked Barry to take him to my apartment. Barry just blew him off, telling him he'd take him later.

"Josh went in his room and waited. At midnight he asked Barry again, but Barry was too wasted to drive. Instead of having one of his friends drive Josh to my apartment, Barry tossed Josh the keys to his truck and told him to drive himself."

What more could he possibly tell me? My mouth was open, my jaw slack. I was waiting for the knockout punch.

I kept looking at Troy. I wanted him to tell me what I thought he was going to tell me hadn't happened.

I couldn't be so lucky.

"Josh got in the truck and drove the four miles to my

apartment," Troy finished. "Do you know how dangerous that was? And how irresponsible of Barry?"

I couldn't even begin to dream of all the consequences.

My twelve-year-old son had driven a truck four miles at midnight. On city streets.

Would the press have had a field day with that had something gone wrong. I imagined the headlines.

Accused Bomber's Son Caught Driving

12-Year-Old John Doe Can Drive

I didn't know what to say.

Josh came in on the tail end of the story and gave Troy a hard look. He didn't want to see Barry get in trouble. To him it was no big deal.

I quietly slipped off into my room and closed the door.

When I woke up, I didn't know if I was in Oklahoma, Nevada, the FBI office, or Decker, Michigan.

In my dreams I'd visited them all. And found peace in none of them.

9

"CALL ME. IT'S URGENT. WE NEED TO TALK ABOUT JOSH."

That's the entire content of the note I wrote to Terry in the middle of October 1994, and in a way, it set off this entire chain of events.

Josh and my current husband, Lee, were into their own version of *Family Feud*, the home game, and tensions were running high. Something always seemed to go wrong between the men I married and my kids.

And it usually wound up with me having to make a choice. When push comes to shove, the fact is that husbands come and go, but you only have one set of kids, if you understand where I'm coming from.

Josh was threatening to run away because of Lee, who had been riding him a bit hard about being overweight and not doing his share to keep the house in order. And I had to admit Josh's room and bathroom were generally an unholy mess.

"I'll go to Michigan and live with Grandma or some other relatives," Josh was now saying defiantly. He had packed some clothes in an old suitcase, and was dead serious about leaving.

"And just how are you going to get there?" I challenged, knowing he was too big for me to confront physically.

"I'll walk if I have to."

"Let's just wait and see what your dad has to say about it," I suggested, trying to make peace. On the one hand, I could see Lee's point, and Josh, like most boys his age, needed to be more mindful about cleaning up after himself. I didn't want to undermine Lee's authority, but on the other hand, I didn't condone the tone he took with Josh.

Problem is, when you're a mother, and a protective one at that, it's hard to just stand by and let things play out. Usually, when situations like this crop up, and they always seem to, I remain calm and try to smooth everyone's ruffled feathers.

This time, though, it got to me.

"I've had it," I screamed at Lee. I then threw not only a fit, but books, a lamp and papers. In retrospect, I know I was responding to more than the incident at hand. It was the buildup of memories lingering from my marriage to Terry and the problems we had had over my son Barry.

Barry was fifteen when he was somehow transformed from "average teenager" into the "teenager from hell." I've got to admit he tried it all. Booze, drugs, stealing money from us, stealing our car. You name it, Barry probably did it.

It was a very tough period in my marriage to Terry, which had begun blissfully and prosperously. My mother was diagnosed with cancer in September of 1984, and I was determined to do all I could to save her. I called the best doctors, inquired about experimental medicines, and even flew to Mexico to buy "miracle drugs" that weren't legal in the United States.

What she appreciated most was my time; every night, I would visit her at the hospital, staying until they made me leave. It meant arriving home after ten every night and, therefore, spending hardly any time with my family, but

Evelyn Dolores Walsh was my family, before any of the others.

At the time of my mother's diagnosis, I had been in insurance sales just six months, and was already the state's number-one producer for AFLAC. My sales and commissions suffered drastically during her illness, but I didn't care.

She lasted almost a year to the day and I was with her almost every night. She died on September 9, 1985. I'll never forget the rainbow that lit up the cloudy sky the morning of her funeral.

Then came Barry's battles with drugs. I finally had to have him committed to Bay Haven Hospital in 1988. And thank God I had insurance, or his confinement might have bankrupted us. Thirty thousand dollars for a month's stay can do considerable damage to most any budget. I had hardly buried my mother when I found myself up to my eyebrows in more emotional trauma.

Playing nursemaid and bad cop to Barry was a full-time job. And more often than not, that job fell to Terry. He was home, I wasn't. I worked fifty miles away, and every night after work for thirty days I attended support meetings for Barry. Terry refused to attend, which didn't make things any easier.

When Barry finished his thirty-day detox, hospital counselors advised me against bringing him home unless he had support from the entire family, including Terry. In truth, Terry tried, but it was hard for him to understand Barry's problems. From Terry's standpoint, if you wanted to stop something, you just made yourself stop.

For my sake, Terry agreed to try.

But Barry was anything but cured. He would borrow the car to go to meetings and come home stoned. He was back doing all the things that had gotten him in trouble in the first place, only he was hiding it better.

The dependency "contract" I had signed with Bay

Haven called for me to use "tough love" and send him away if he violated his part of the bargain and fell off the wagon. When he did, I kicked him out, changed the locks, and sent him to his father's. But I'd always relent and allow him back. I was no help to either of us.

One night Terry and I were lying in bed when suddenly he sat straight up. He startled me.

"Are you okay?" I asked, hoping he wasn't ill.

"The kid's no good," he said, referring to Barry. "You have to face the fact he isn't going to change. He's a bad influence on the other kids."

How could anyone be saying that about the boy I had named after Barry Manilow?

"One of us has to go. Either Barry goes or I'm leaving." It was the spring of 1986. My mother hadn't been dead a year, I was in danger of losing my oldest son to drugs, and my husband was threatening to leave me. Wasn't life grand?

"I love you both," I said, tears trickling down my cheeks in the dark. "I can't make that decision." Thing was, I knew Terry was a good stepparent. He cared about the kids, including Barry. It was just that he was a perfectionist and had a hard time accepting a problem he couldn't control. I was sympathetic to Terry's feelings, but this was my son.

From this point on, our relationship deteriorated. The next two years were a struggle, for both of us. Terry seemed lost. In a way, he battled with life. I guess it was just a matter of time until we drifted apart.

In 1987, our marriage was at its lowest point, which was in direct contrast to my career, which was going great guns. I had won a car in 1984 for outstanding sales performance and in 1987 won a trip to Las Vegas. Terry had no interest in coming along. He had taken a job at UPS for the Christmas season and was up to his boots in packages.

We talked about it but neither of us had a solution. And neither of us really wanted to say the "D" word.

Then, in 1988, we couldn't pretend anymore. The rental property we had purchased, and which Terry repaired, using his carpentry and handyman skills, and the penny stocks, the gold and silver futures, and my success were not enough to fight off talk of a separation and possible divorce.

Terry was becoming more and more of a basket case and I was worried about him. I even feared he might commit suicide. I knew he needed a purpose in life, something to believe in and something to care about.

One afternoon, as I prepared to leave the building where my office was located, I stopped by the U.S. Army field office on the first floor and picked up one of their recruiting brochures.

I laid it on our oak table, and when I came back through the kitchen, the pamphlet was gone.

For the next two weeks Terry whipped himself into shape. He ran, did sit-ups and push-ups, and practiced shooting every day to improve his marksmanship. He had made up his mind. There was nothing left for him in our marriage and his life was on a treadmill. He was going to join the army, and he wanted to be ready.

Two weeks later our separation became official when Terry joined the service and left for basic training in Fort Benning, Georgia. It was May 24, 1988. He was thirty-three, just two years below the maximum age for enlisting. We both cried very hard the night before he left for the army. The thing is, we weren't angry at each other. Our marriage was just broken and we didn't know how to fix it.

"I don't care what you do, as long as you're happy," I said as I held his head in my lap. He was sobbing, and I'm sure uncertainty about his decision and the breakup of his family were weighing heavily on his mind.

By some twisted stroke of fate, a skinny, stone-faced kid was joining up the same day in Buffalo, New York. His name was Tim McVeigh and he, too, was headed to Fort Benning.

The incongruous duo would become fast friends on the rifle range; they shared an interest in guns and were often seen poring over survivalist-type magazines. Both were assigned to Fort Riley, Kansas, where, despite being in different companies, their friendship blossomed.

Josh had remained with me while Terry was in basic training, but when he settled in at Fort Riley, he came and got his son. They rented a house off the base and eventually took in a boarder, a woman named Linda, and her son. It was a business arrangement. She got free room and board in exchange for taking care of Josh while Terry was on duty.

Troy and I remained on our eighty-acre farm in Snover. Troy continued attending Cass City High while Barry, who had been kicked out, was supposed to be staying with his father. However, I knew that wasn't happening. My sources told me he was crashing at whatever friend's house he could find.

My heart broke for him, but I had to be strong enough not to let him come back and take advantage of me. And Terry had mainly taken Josh so he wouldn't fall under Barry's influence.

In November 1988, I filed for divorce in Sanilac County, Michigan. A summons was sent to Terry at Fort Riley. After initially adjusting to army life quite well, he was, at this time, beginning to have a tougher time. Shortly after enlisting he was made a platoon leader, but a prank he and McVeigh pulled didn't sit well with ranking officers and his leadership status had been rescinded.

On May 12, 1989, my petition for divorce was dismissed,

supposedly because some court papers were not properly filed. I still believe it was because I had not fulfilled the necessary residency requirement.

Three days later, on May 15, Terry was granted a hardship discharge from the army. I've always wondered just why he was released, less than a year after enlisting, and always been told it was because he had to take care of Josh. But this theory never washed with me because he'd had Josh with him all along. I really believe Josh was just a convenient excuse and that Terry had become disillusioned with the army because he believed he would never rise through the ranks.

When Terry was discharged, I agreed to let him have the house and acreage in Snover, provided Troy was allowed to stay and live with him. I moved to Bay City, where I rented a room. It was more convenient for us all because I was closer to my work and the boys could live in the environment they were used to.

Then, in October 1989, I made up my mind to move to Las Vegas. It seemed like a city of excitement, and unlimited opportunity in the real-estate business. I was confident I could be successful in Nevada and so I packed everything I could in my car and hit the road.

If my life had been reduced to a personals ad, it might have read: "Independent, thirty-something farm girl w/big-city dreams. Confident, capable, and in search of adventure."

Although our divorce still wasn't final and I don't think either of us had second thoughts, we nevertheless saw each other in November of 1989 when Terry brought Josh to Las Vegas. At first, I wondered if he was going to try for a reconciliation, but Terry not only didn't try to kiss and make up, he showed no interest at all, which was fine with me. I had definitely come to the conclusion that the marriage was over, even though I still loved him.

On the surface his reason for coming was to give Josh and me a chance to visit, but he had an ulterior motive as well. He was headed for the Philippines for a short vacation. It was a place he'd never been before, and Terry was never one to take vacations. It was odd, but I didn't care what his real reason was.

When he returned in late November, Terry surprised me by urging me to get our divorce finalized. "I've met someone I want to marry," he said shyly.

I couldn't have been more stunned if he had told me he'd won the lottery.

"She's a young Filipino girl," was the only explanation he offered. "I met her in Cebu." I didn't ask how or why, but sometime later his bride's age came up and I asked about it.

"Why so young?" he repeated smugly. "I suppose because young ones are easier to train."

In mid-December 1989, I flew from Vegas to spend Christmas with my family in Michigan. And on December 18, I appeared in court, where our divorce decree was granted. Our property was split fairly equally, with Terry keeping the house in Snover and me getting title to some other properties. It was also agreed that Troy would be allowed to continue living with Terry and attending Cass City High School.

We were given joint custody of Josh, with Terry retaining physical custody. I also agreed to pay $200-per-month child support, which may sound unusual, but I had the greater income and wanted to provide for my son, too. Terry didn't appear in court.

It was a far cry from 1983, when we were very happy and very much in love. That was the year Terry and I took a trip to San Diego to visit my aunt, then down to Newport Beach to meet the stockbroker we'd been dealing with over the telephone for a year. Finally, at my request, we made a side trip to Las Vegas. Terry had no interest in going to Vegas, but I'd never been there and he indulged me.

We stayed at Sam's Town, one of the favorite casinos for locals, and we had a great time. We didn't gamble, but we made love, enjoyed the restaurants, and were fascinated by the excitement.

It was fun.

Terry even mentioned owning property in Vegas. We rented a car from a friendly man named Bobby Page at Dollar Rent-A-Car and drove from one end of town to the other. We explored.

That was then, this was now.

It was now October 1994, we had been divorced for years, and his son needed him.

Now Josh was seemingly at a crossroads and the man who could do something about it was nowhere to be found.

Terry had been traipsing back and forth across the country for the past six months, taking advantage of the fact that Marife was back in school in the Philippines, and perhaps, trying to lose the feelings of despondency he felt over Jason's death. He and Marife had settled in Vegas between December 1993 and April 1994, residing in the single-story Duck Creek condos behind a power plant in the southeast section of town, but even during these four months, he commuted to Kansas, often staying at the Dreamland Motel in Junction City.

He told friends he was trying to set himself up in the military-hardware-and-surplus business. Apparently he was also looking for other work, because in March he answered a newspaper ad for a farmhand.

Terry went to work for owner Jim Donahue on the Hayhook Ranch in Marion, Kansas, where he, Marife, and Nicole lived in a small house. Donahue remembers him as a good worker, "even though he knew more about machinery than livestock."

Having given thirty days' notice, Terry quit the Donahue farm on September 1. He had saved $12,000 and Marife was ready to go back to the Philippines to begin the school year. Terry made plans to join her in November, with the idea of staying in Cebu City permanently.

During the time Terry lived in Vegas, I had hoped he would settle down so he could spend a lot of time with Josh, and for a while it worked. They saw each other every day. He had tried Vegas a couple years before, and I thought it would work out, but it fizzled. Marife had gotten a job as a waitress in a Filipino restaurant, and Terry worked there for a short time as some sort of security guard or bouncer. Occasionally I baby-sat Nicole when they both worked.

He had even enrolled in a slot mechanics school in 1991 and was just a few weeks short of completing it when his mother called, saying she needed him to help with the farm. As always, he complied with her wishes. Terry was a surer bet to go home when Mommy called than the swallows were to return to Capistrano. He dropped out of the slot school, without a certificate, even though he had already paid the full tuition, packed up Marife, Josh, and Jason and made tracks for Michigan.

He didn't care that he was breaking his year lease on the condo.

After leaving Vegas in 1993 for Michigan and then moving to Kansas, Terry was now on the road with his old army buddy Tim McVeigh, traveling to gun shows to buy, sell, and trade weapons and surplus stuff. Since he had no permanent address, the only way I could contact him was by writing to a post office box in Marion, Kansas.

I hadn't seen him since the first week of October when he came to visit Josh for a couple days before continuing on to Kingman, Arizona. Josh was very sad and agitated when his dad left. He felt unwanted. He had always been a major part of Terry's life. Now, instead of being able to talk to him, I had to wait for him to get my letter and call back.

Two weeks later he called.

The crisis period was over. Josh had backed down from his threats of running away and was generally behaving himself. Still, I let Terry have it.

"I can't believe it took two damn weeks for you to call," I said loudly. "Do you know how ridiculous that is, Terry? Can't you just stop and stay in one place for the next five years and raise your son? You know how much he loves you and how much he misses you."

"You just don't understand, Lana. . . . " Terry protested.

"I understand enough to know this isn't what I bargained for. I understand enough to know that you had committed to raising Josh and you're not doing it. I understand enough to know that when either of us needs to talk to you, we can't. Instead we have to write to some stupid post office box and hope you get the letter."

Terry was impatient. He didn't appreciate being scolded. "You have no idea what's going on," he told me. "People are getting fed up with everything from welfare to the government. There's some big changes coming in this country."

"Right, Terry. And what are you going to do, start a revolt? That guy who was shooting at the White House was fed up, too. Do you think that's the way to handle things?"

"That guy wasn't all wrong, Lana. The government is the problem. You've got to see that."

"Whatever you say, Terry. In the meantime I don't have time to listen to all this crap. I wrote you about your son. He's having a very hard time. He's threatened to run away, he's moody, and he's unhappy. He's always wondering where you are, or wanting to talk to you. It would be nice if you could come back as soon as possible and have a talk with him. Spend some quality time with him."

"I'll get there as soon as I can, Lana," he promised.

"And when will that be?"

"Probably the first week of November. That's only about ten days from now." He never mentioned his plans to travel and possibly move to the Philippines in November.

"That'll be fine. I'll tell Josh. And I'll talk to Lee about you sleeping on the couch. I don't think it will be a problem." I knew how frugal he was. Terry would sleep in his truck in front of the house rather than spend the money for a motel, so putting him up would be easier. I would never have been able to explain to Josh why his dad had to sleep in his truck anyway.

Terry seemed different, even a little weird, on the phone, and some of the things he ranted about made absolutely no sense to me. The conversation, however, did make me think about the Terry Nichols I once knew.

It's funny how it all started.

I mean, for some couples it's love at first sight. For others it's lust at first glance. For Terry and me, it was more a case of being in the right place at the right time.

I was twice divorced, although my second marriage hardly counts since it only lasted six months, and I was living on a small ranch house in Decker, Michigan, the first time I ever laid eyes on Terry Lynn Nichols. He was twenty-six, thin, clean-cut, and friendly. And he was sitting erect and proud in the driver's seat of a John Deere tractor, farming the land adjacent to my house.

I was thirty-one, full of life, and maybe one of the most successful woman real estate and life-insurance professionals in the county. I was also enjoying my freedom. I loved men, but didn't really need one. Especially any resembling the two I'd had.

I'm not exactly sure how we started talking, or who initiated the conversation, but I do remember that it was about real estate. Terry was interested in buying some property in the area and thought I might be the person to help.

It was the first of many business deals we made together. Terry closed a deal on 120 acres in March of 1980. We continued to see each other, and while the relationship wasn't one of white-hot passion, handholding turned into petting, which turned into intimacy, and by 1981 we were married.

But we didn't have his mother's blessing. In fact, Terry feared Joyce Wilt would disown him. Instead of a fancy wedding, we eloped to the county courthouse in Caro, Michigan.

For the next year or so Joyce Wilt turned her back on both of us, speaking to Terry only when she couldn't avoid it. She didn't start to thaw until Josh was born in August of 1982.

More than anything else, life threw a pretty serious roadblock in the path of Terry and me having a storybook life. The "happily-ever-afters" in the fairy tales don't reckon with a terminally ill parent, a son addicted to drugs, and a husband and wife with different motivational drives and different needs. And usually, neither Prince Charming nor the luscious maiden is lugging any baggage from a previous marriage or has an overbearing mother-in-law.

If nothing else, I'd like people to understand that Terry and I once really loved each other. He didn't want to leave and I didn't really want to see him go.

Maybe that's why we never really broke it off and remained on good terms, with a special place in each of our hearts for the other.

Circumstances just got in the way.

10

COMPARED WITH APRIL AND MAY, JUNE WAS A slow month. It was a month during which I desperately wanted to play "Let's Pretend."

Let's Pretend we're a normal family. Let's Pretend we don't have a relative implicated in the worst terrorist attack in American history. Let's Pretend reporters aren't calling us every few minutes, and Let's Pretend people aren't pointing at us in stores and recognizing us from our pictures in the paper.

Let's Pretend we can have our lives back. The ones we had before April 21.

Funny, the things you remember sometimes.

I remember my birthday, April 18. I worked all day, then had a small party in the evening. Just the kids and some friends, a cake, and pizza. Terry called in the middle of it all, about 8:00 P.M., to check on Josh, who had arrived at 1:00 A.M. He wanted to be sure the flight had gone smoothly and to make small talk with his son.

I remember telling Josh to take the phone in the bedroom so he could hear better, because Terry speaks very softly. I didn't know it would be the last time he'd speak to his dad for a long time.

April 19, I was driving to work when I heard a news report about the bombing. I was shocked and angry.

What kind of person could do something like that? I thought. It must have been the same terrorists who blew up that building in New York.

On April 20, I was at my dentist's office. I was in an unflattering position with the chair tilted back, cotton in my mouth, and under the influence of nerve gas. The voices were faint, as if coming from a distance, but I could still distinguish the words. Dr. Montgomery and his nurse were discussing the bombing and I heard them say a report on the radio had claimed the attack was carried out by two Americans. How could that be? I remember wondering. How could anyone be heartless enough to kill innocent children?

April 21 would have been my mother's birthday. It was also the day the FBI came to my office and took my life away.

Now it was June.

From a media standpoint, there wasn't a lot happening. The government was fairly quiet, Terry's attorneys weren't making statements, and the bombing had slipped off the front pages of America's newspapers.

Things slowed down for Josh and me, too, but we were still being swept along, like twigs in a powerful flash flood. In the first part of the month my divorce from Lee became final. It had been pending for a couple months, so it came as no surprise. It was just that with everything else going on, there was no good time for it. I was sorry it hadn't worked out, but I was too old to put in a lot of time fighting for something against long odds. In the past few years I adopted the philosophy of moving on if something wasn't right.

I even responded to a call from some private investigator out of Oklahoma. He claimed to be working in tandem with a reporter from Channel 4 television in Oklahoma City, and said he had knowledge of a conspiracy and proof that foreign terrorists had actually been behind the bombing and that Terry was being set up.

This, of course, piqued my interest. The investigator, one Robert Jerlow, asked if he could come to the house to interview me. I asked Andy what he thought, and he said the whole story sounded bogus. No newspapers had given credence to the information Jerlow was claiming to have. Andy insisted I have nothing to do with Jerlow or Channel 4, saying he didn't trust them. "They're just trying to get an exclusive interview with you," he warned.

Unbeknownst to Andy, I agreed to meet Jerlow anyway. I wanted to know more about his theory. To see the pictures of "Mr. Big" he claimed to have and get a feel for the whole thing.

I met him and a wispy, black-haired reporter named Jayna Davis at the Sands Hotel coffee shop. Andy was wrong. They didn't ask for an interview and had no cameras or microphones. I was relieved. No harm could come of the clandestine meeting, and no one had to know about it.

The meeting lasted about forty-five minutes, with the three of us exchanging theories and "what-ifs," them picking my brain and I theirs. They told me the government was interested in their information, and they'd been summoned to the Pentagon to talk about the foreign-terrorist theory the following week.

"People in Washington are very interested in seeing these pictures," said Jerlow, alluding to the photos spread out on the table. He passed copies of a few to me. "Show these to Josh and see if he recognizes anyone," he said. "One of them is Mr. Big. He comes to Vegas once a month, always has ten thousand or more in his pocket, and is connected to a foreign government. Just show them to Josh."

Stan had been working on arranging for Josh and me

to go see Terry. Finally we got a letter from the prison naming me as an authorized visitor. Oddly, the memo from the warden's office didn't mention Josh, although he was the one the visit was all about.

It took another week and a second letter before we received notification that Josh was also on Terry's approved-visitor list. That left one major stumbling block. Josh wanted a contact visit. He wanted to be able to give his dad a hug.

I thought this was a reasonable request considering Terry had not been convicted of a crime and, in fact, at the time had not even been charged with the bombing. He was basically being held as a material witness, although no one doubted he would be charged any day.

Still, other prisoners at El Reno, men convicted of crimes ranging from robbery and rape to murder, were allowed contact, even conjugal visits. Why couldn't this man, who was not yet convicted, hug his only son? The more I thought about it, the more worked up I got.

Stan inferred from the tone of the warden's letter that a contact visit was highly unlikely. We told Josh it was being discussed. I didn't want to give him a definite thumbs-down because I didn't want to dampen his spirits about seeing his dad.

I had agonized for days over the appropriateness of a visit at all. Was it better for him to see his dad, even if he had to see him in prison, or would it be better to spare Josh the pain and keep him away?

Josh was not going to be denied. Terry Nichols was his father and he didn't care if he had to scale a mountain to see him for only a moment. To Josh, the where of it did not matter.

Personally, I dreaded returning to Oklahoma, but we made plans to go over the Fourth of July holiday. We'd stay from Tuesday through Friday and visit Terry every day for a couple of hours.

Father's Day, June 18, was another emotional day. Weren't they all?

Josh had paced around the house waiting for his dad to call. Finally, late in the afternoon, he pestered me to call the prison to see if they'd let him talk to his dad. I knew it would be futile, but I did it anyway, to appease him.

We reached an assistant warden, who advised us Terry's calls were restricted, which we knew, and that if he was allowed to make any calls that day, who he called would be strictly up to Mr. Nichols. The conversation was amicable, but certainly not warm.

Father's Day was a day to remember for another reason as well. Without looking for it, we found more trouble waiting for us, and in a very unlikely place.

I drove Josh to a new amusement/theme park on Sunset Road around one o'clock, hoping that getting out of the house might help. As he got out of the passenger-side of the car, something a couple spaces over caught his eye. He moseyed down to see what it was and came eyeball to eyeball with a bleeding man lying on the pavement.

Someone from the park was running toward the scene screaming that he'd called the police.

Josh stared at the man for another second or two then hurried back to our car. "There's a dead guy over there," he said excitedly. "Looks like he's been shot."

"Let's get the hell out of here," I said, zipping my LeBaron into reverse. As I was backing out, a Mercy ambulance paramedic vehicle, with sirens blaring, swerved right behind me. I let it go past and turned to head out the driveway.

Just then, a Henderson police car flashed in, passing right next to me.

"That's all we needed," I said to Josh, "was for you to have been the one to find the body. We didn't need you to be in the newspaper again."

"He really was dead, Mom. I wonder what happened."

"We don't need to know," I told him. And suddenly it seemed like everywhere we went, tragedy followed, and everything we touched turned to horror.

A story in the next day's newspaper said the man had been shot by his ex-girlfriend, who was upset over his requests for visitation rights with their child. Now the baby would have no mother or father.

I started going into the office for a couple hours a day near the end of June, but I was nonfunctional. All I really did was sit there. After an hour or so, I'd leave crying. Two of our key insurance agents quit during that time, and we lost a couple others who were concerned about how the bombing would reflect on them.

"Some realtors are calling us the 'terrorist office,'" one of the defecting agents told me. "Your ex-husband being involved in the bombing and all the publicity you've gotten have hurt us. I just want to make a change."

In late June, reports about Michael Fortier reaching a plea bargain with the government began to surface.

Fortier had supposedly admitted to having cased the federal building with Tim McVeigh months earlier and had other information that could tie McVeigh to the crime. Not much was said about whether or not he had mentioned Terry. Everything we heard indicated that Fortier was rolling over to solidify the case against McVeigh.

It was another sliver of hope that maybe Terry was not a key player.

I was mildly surprised when Josh asked if Andy could come with us on the trip to El Reno, but I had no real objections. Josh had developed a strong attachment to Andy and I think he wanted him along for moral support as well as companionship.

Meanwhile Stan had received another letter from the warden, this one explaining prison rules and why Josh wouldn't be allowed to have a contact visit, and I had it in my purse as the three of us boarded the flight.

Josh was edgy and full of nervous energy on the leg from Las Vegas to Phoenix, and I think even he realized he was being a nuisance.

When we reboarded after the short stopover, Josh found a seat on the aisle in the front section of the cabin, far away from Andy and my seats. He isn't bashful, and has no trouble striking up a conversation with strangers.

It was the Fourth of July. The rest of the country was celebrating its freedom, but we were no longer free. We were prisoners of circumstance.

Andy thought it would be better to find a motel in El Reno instead of having to commute from Oklahoma City to the prison every day. He had booked us into a Best Western less than five miles from the prison and arranged a rental car. Josh and I had a room with two double beds. Andy was next door. All of our rooms overlooked the pool.

It was Tuesday midafternoon by the time we got situated in the hotel, so instead of trying to fight through the red tape only to spend a few minutes with Terry, we decided to get an early start on Wednesday. I was mentally prepared for the worst, and had some apprehensions about seeing Terry.

Of course I was curious about his mental state and health, but I wondered what his attitude would be toward me since he probably knew I had turned over the letters to the FBI.

Josh was somewhat sedate and wasn't joking around like he usually did. I knew inside he was a bundle of emotion.

We were at the prison by 8:55 A.M., intending to stay until about noon, because we were told his attorneys would want to see him in the afternoon. The warden's letter had contained a printed sheet of instructions and I had adhered to them. No shorts, no provocative clothing, only a clear purse, etc.

Andy turned into the wide entryway, stopping when an armed security guard flagged us down. He asked our names and the nature of our business then directed us to a guard booth about sixty yards behind him. Huge loops of barbed wire rose above the long expanse of fence surrounding the prison.

The area would not likely be mistaken for a campground.

A mile or so before reaching the prison, large, boldly printed highway signs warned against picking up hitchhikers. PERSONS HITCHHIKING ALONG THIS HIGHWAY MAY BE ESCAPED PRISONERS. There were small farms and pretty green fields along the way, then suddenly the huge prison loomed on our left. It was set far back from the road.

Andy dropped us in front of the guard booth, made a U-turn, and headed back for the hotel. Josh and I were detained and searched in the booth where we were told to wait and that someone would come and escort us to Terry.

We waited more than an hour, and did not find out until the next day that the holdup was due to something going on with Tim McVeigh and his attorney that required the presence of the assistant warden. That delay cut our visiting time with Terry down to about an hour, and all of us were disappointed.

The visit was noncontact. Terry was in a room, separated from us by a Plexiglas shield. He appeared thin and nervous. His eyes were wide and he avoided looking at me directly. He was happy to see Josh, but humbled by the circumstance. Terry was also amazed at how big Josh had gotten in the three months since he'd seen him.

I'm sure Josh noticed the stress on his dad's face, but it didn't faze him. He chatted with his dad, even trying to talk to him about sports, something Josh loved and followed closely, but in which Terry had little interest.

"How are you?" I asked. "Are they treating you all right? Are you eating?"

"I'm as well as can be expected," he said, looking to the side. A guard stood a few yards away. "I'm eating. They feed me plenty. The food just isn't very good." He expressed concern over Marife, wondering if we'd seen or talked to her, and told us that the main reading he'd done was the Bible. He said he'd read the whole thing from cover to cover.

"All twelve hundred pages," he said with a smile.

And then it was over. The guard said time was up and we said good-bye with our eyes. He turned and walked away.

On our way out of the prison we met a couple of Terry's lawyers. We introduced ourselves and I told them where we were staying. They asked if they could come by for a few minutes after they finished visiting Terry.

I said I'd be waiting.

Attorney Ron Woods and an investigator who worked with him, a man named H.C., came by the hotel later in the afternoon. Josh went swimming while I chatted with them. It was informal, and mainly informational, and they reminded me there were areas we couldn't get into because my lawyer wasn't present.

It surprised me to learn that they knew very little about me and didn't even know that my sister and I had each married a Nichols brother. I hoped they would do a lot more investigating, and do it more thoroughly, if they intended to give Terry decent representation.

They did advise that we limit the areas of conversation with Terry and that I not ask him any specific questions about the case, because our visit and conversation were being monitored. "Things have a way of being twisted around and taken out of context," one of them said, and I understood exactly what he meant.

Still, I would have liked to ask Terry straight out what the hell was going on. I wanted to say, "If you know anything, why don't you just come clean, and maybe they'll go easy on you." I so badly wanted to know the truth.

Our second day's visit, on Thursday, was a bit boring because I had to remind myself not to ask certain questions. Even Josh was a little bored. I think his main questions had been answered just seeing his dad. He knew he was alive and well. He wanted to hug him badly, and had asked again when the assistant warden led us to the meeting room, but he was gently rebuffed.

He told his dad he loved him a hundred times, talked about sports, his friends, Marife, and being out of school. And they sat and looked at each other for long minutes, both at a loss for words, neither wanting to cry, and tears in both of their eyes. I couldn't watch. We left again at noon, but this time we had had a full three hours.

I had arranged to meet with the private investigator, Jerlow, and Jayna Davis in the Best Western coffee shop at 2:30. I had intended for just Josh and me to go, but it would have been impossible to slip away without Andy knowing. So I told him.

"How did they know you were here?" he asked.

"I called them yesterday," I said, not afraid that he would be disappointed. "I told you they were okay people."

Then I decided to tell the whole truth. "I met with them last month at the Sands in Las Vegas. There were no cameras. They just had some questions and they have some interesting theories. I want to follow through with them. They might be onto something. You don't have to be there. I can handle it. I trust them."

"If you're meeting them, I'm going with you," he said, resigned but peeved.

Josh, Andy, and I walked across the quaint little wooden bridge connecting the motel to the coffee shop and found a booth in the back. A few minutes later Jerlow and Jayna Davis entered and made their way back to us. Introductions were made all around since neither Josh nor Andy had met them before.

They were excited, Andy was silent and moody. When one of them presented a theory about a government cover-up and foreign terrorists being behind the bombing, Andy attacked, questioning both their theory and their credibility, and I got hot.

"You have a lousy attitude Andy," I reprimanded. "Why are you so negative?"

"That's okay," Davis answered, trying to keep peace. "I understand."

"I'm negative because I think they're hustlers and they're full of crap," said Andy, more vociferous than I'd ever seen him. "If their theory is so plausible, why is it no one else in the country is pursuing it? Do you really think CNN, *The New York Times, Time,* and all the networks have missed it and these two guys are the only people smart enough to see the conspiracy?

"How can you be so naive, Lana?"

"Even my police friends won't talk to me," Jerlow answered, going on to say he'd welcome the chance for federal officials to acknowledge him and disprove his theory. "I wish they would so I could get back to what I usually do, handling insurance cases."

"I just think you're two small-time reporters looking for a story so you can move up the food chain," Andy said meanly. "I think you're trying to use these two people and I don't like it."

"How are they trying to use us?" I asked. "We haven't done anything for them except look at a few pictures."

"It's just a feeling I have after thirty-plus years in the

news business," Andy said. "I don't feel comfortable with this. I know the government would like nothing better than to prove this act of terrorism was committed by foreigners, so they'd have no reason to cover that up."

Andy was trying to be softer, but he was still steamed.

Jerlow pushed some pictures over to Josh. "Does anyone seem familiar to you?" he asked, hoping Josh would reply in the affirmative.

Josh shook his head. "Not really. Although this guy looks a little like someone I've seen on television."

"What do you think of when you see him?"

"He looks mean."

"Evil?"

"I guess."

At 5:30, we drove a few miles down the road to meet Terry's team of lawyers at the Outback Steakhouse. His lead attorney, Michael Tigar, was not present, but Woods, H.C., two other female attorneys, and an aide were all present and accounted for.

I had no appetite.

There were so many things I wanted to ask them about, but protocol dictated I act like a lady and not ask. They would probably not have answered me anyway, and they would have left wondering why Terry Nichols's ex-wife was so pushy and so hell-bent on solving the case.

They might also have formed the opinion that I was a loose cannon. I had just enough information to be dangerous. Besides, why would they want to tell me anything? At the moment I was on the prosecution witness list, which technically made me an enemy.

But I saw myself as neutral. I was no one's witness. I was only going to tell the truth.

On Friday, Andy dropped us off at El Reno at 8:55 again, then went into downtown Oklahoma City to tour the remains of the federal building at Fifth and Robinson. A two-block square area had been fenced off around the Murrah site, and the chain-link fences were laden with flowers, wreaths, and cards from well-wishers. Security guards patrolled every entrance.

Our last visit with Terry was sad.

He told us he'd received a letter from an Oklahoma City insurance adjuster with a bill for $1,300. "That's for damages to a nearby building," he said evenly.

There was sadness in his eyes, and I had no way of knowing if it was because it was our final visit, or if it was because he wanted to talk to us but couldn't because of the security.

When the visit was over, the assistant warden came in to escort us back to the main guard booth. Josh whirled and looked him right in the eye. He was almost as tall as the man in the brown suit.

"Can I just please give my dad one hug before we go?" he begged.

I thought for a second the official was going to break down. He could see the longing in Josh's face, and Terry could hear the conversation. Instead of just turning and walking off, Terry lingered. He, too, was hoping.

"I'm afraid not, son. Prison rules."

"What would it hurt?" Josh asked again. "Besides, you make the rules."

"This is a noncontact visit," the warden said, reverting to safer ground. "I'm very sorry."

You bastard, I thought. It wouldn't have hurt to give the kid a break.

Terry told us he had a letter from Marife. He was going to open it when he got back to his cell.

I had a hunch I knew what it said. She had called me in Las Vegas and casually mentioned that she was thinking of asking Terry for a divorce. It would probably mean he would never get a chance to see his unborn child, because once she went back to the Philippines, I didn't think she'd return unless she was ordered to for the trial.

Funny how it turned out. Terry had once told a neighbor that one of the most important things in life for him was to have a faithful wife. Someone who would always stand by his side. Marife's infidelity and the possibility that she might leave him in the lurch now would both weigh heavily on his mind.

His lawyers had already told us they were going to keep an extra-close eye on him after we left, because they figured he would be very distraught. With Marife's news, he was going to be a basket case. The prison had him under twenty-four-hour video surveillance, which, under the present circumstance, was a good thing. Someone needed to keep an eye on him.

We had a long, fairly silent trip home, all of us caught up in our own private thoughts.

It wasn't until the following Tuesday that the adventure picked up again.

That's when a reporter from Oklahoma called to ask about the interview I'd done with Channel 4 in Oklahoma.

"What interview?" I asked, completely baffled.

Those lowlife slime Jerlow and Davis had used a hidden lipstick camera to record our meeting at the Sands Hotel, and even though the picture quality was weak, the station aired it in three segments over two days. They clipped and edited it in a manner that members of the mainstream press found appalling and underhanded. The station justified its actions with a disclaimer stating that they were forced to get the interview using secret tactics because I refused to do any interviews unless I was I compensated.

It was a blatant lie. I had done interviews with CNN, *PrimeTime*, the *Las Vegas Review-Journal*, the Associated

Press, and a number of other reputable news media without ever discussing money.

Andy had been right all along. Channel 4 had their little exclusive scoop and I had been their unsuspecting patsy.

I couldn't have felt any more violated if I had been raped.

11

I TRIED TO MASK MY FRUSTRATION AND DISAP-
pointment on the way home from El Reno, but it was
very difficult.

I mean, I understood that Terry's lawyers didn't want
him to discuss the case, but if he was innocent, what
could it have hurt for him to say to his son "I didn't do it.
This is all some sort of mix-up. It will all be straightened
out pretty soon"?

How could his saying he was innocent have been mis-
construed? It would have been important for me to hear
those words, too. I wanted desperately to believe in his
innocence, but I needed his help.

I wanted Terry to speak out. Tim McVeigh had. He
and his lawyer had gone on record in a "limited" question-and-answer interview with *Newsweek*.

There he was, mugging for the cameras, being coy and
trying to be personable. Smugly smiling at America from
the cover. It was a calculated gamble by his attorney,
Steven Jones.

Since his arrest, McVeigh had been portrayed as a
stone-faced, sullen prisoner who had given nothing but
his name, rank, serial number, and a statement that he
was a political prisoner of war. This tactic had convinced
the country that he was guilty and had something to hide.

He had no family. No children. He was a loner. Background stories on McVeigh always portrayed him as angry, a demolitions man in the army and a government hater. Terry, on the other hand, had been painted as a family man. He had recently bought a house, had a wife and child and friends who spoke about him being a gentle, caring man. No one stepped forward to make similar claims about McVeigh.

So now the worm was trying to turn.

The world had seen, or at least been told, about McVeigh's dark side. Now it was going to get a different spin. The soft side. The human side.

It made me sick.

Asked by *Newsweek* if he, Terry, and Michael Fortier were close friends, he said yes.

Asked if he and Terry played with demolitions on the farm, McVeigh's answer was a little evasive. "It would amount to firecrackers," he said. "They were plastic Pepsi bottles that burst because of air pressure. It was like popping a paper bag."

He made it sound harmless.

He went on to deny having just given his name, rank, and serial number and to say he was horrified when he learned of the deaths of the children in the bombing. In a smooth public-relations move, he also downplayed his anger over the Waco siege, claiming only that he "was bothered by it."

Asked if he committed the crime, McVeigh would only say, "We are going to plead not guilty."

Told it was an opportunity for him to say "Hell no, I didn't do it," McVeigh responded, "We can't do that." And Jones jumped in with, "And if he says 'Hell no,' the government isn't just going to say, 'Well okay, that settles that.'"

Okay, America, that's Tim McVeigh. Look at the pictures. Contemplative, with his hands on his temples, full face smiling and a pensive profile view. You wonder how many they had to take before they got the ones that appeared. And did he or his lawyer have approval over the pictures or the copy?

I was willing to bet Tim's attorney would have insisted on final approval of the story. *Newsweek* would probably insist otherwise, but with the stakes so high, that seemed a good bet.

But then, what did they have to lose? He was already seen as something subhuman, the lowest life-form. A mass murderer and a killer of innocent children. A coward hated by millions who didn't even know him.

Ross Perot, never one to miss an opportunity to speak out, had said, "These people need to be tried, sentenced, and executed pretty fast. And that kind of clears your head. That worked in the Old West, and it'll work today." He was probably expressing a sentiment shared by many Americans.

But I could see what was happening. They were going to try to make America feel sorry for Tim and they were going to try to dump the whole thing on Terry. Make him the mastermind. Make McVeigh out to be the little Boy Scout who was led astray by an older, wiser man he trusted and looked up to.

Terry had to say something. He had to come out of his cocoon. I wasn't his lawyer, and I know little if anything about legal strategy, but the way I saw it, the general public might actually start to sympathize with McVeigh. They might also start to find it easier to believe Terry was the man behind the whole plot if he continued to remain silent while mountains of evidence against him appeared in the newspapers every day.

It didn't matter that almost everything that was printed or said was speculative. The fact was, none of it was being rebutted. Terry's camp was silent. Deadly silent.

Was there a side to Terry Nichols I didn't know?

A *New York Times* article claimed he "led a double life. On the surface he appeared to be the same old Terry Nichols—quiet, nondescript and not particularly successful. A man trying to hold his family together as he made yet another new start in Kansas." It went on to say, "But if the affidavits are to be believed, Terry Nichols was a man on a secret mission, a bomb builder who used a string of aliases as he went about methodically amassing 4,000 pounds of ammonium nitrate fertilizer, ground ammonium nitrate and diesel fuel—the ingredients of a fertilizer bomb—in rented storage lockers across Kansas."

The story finished with an underhanded dig, claiming that if "Terry Nichols did join McVeigh in constructing the bomb that destroyed the Federal Building, it may have been the only plan of action he had ever carried through, from beginning to end."

Could one year in the army have transformed Terry's life that much?

I knew that a couple years after leaving the army, Terry had tried to renounce his citizenship. He sent a letter to the county clerk in Michigan, along with his voter registration card, saying "the entire political system from the local government on up through the president of the United States [was] corrupt." That's when he declared himself a "nonresident alien nonforeigner and a stranger to the current state of the forum." It was a language familiar to right-wing extremists.

Each day, as I went through the newspapers with my morning coffee, what most concerned me were articles intimating that Terry and McVeigh might have been connected to a string of unsolved bank robberies throughout the Midwest. A Washington bureau reporter quoted some investigators as saying the robberies "appeared to have been committed by a small group of people matching the bombing suspects' general description."

The thirteen heists had begun in Ames, Iowa, on January 25, 1994, and they all fit the same pattern. Each involved two or three white men dressed as construction workers wearing hard hats, gloves, and camouflage netting over their faces. Sometimes they wore masks. Usually they left behind something that looked like a bomb.

The robbers also displayed a certain flair for comedy, adding Santa Claus hats to their wardrobes in December when they robbed an Ohio bank.

"Yes," I exclaimed loudly, banging my hand on the table when I read about the Christmas holdup.

That was a point for Terry, and a big one.

There was no way he could have been involved in a December 1994 robbery in Ohio because he was in the Philippines at the time.

But if the bank robberies weren't the way the bombers financed their deadly mission, how did they do it? Investigators were checking every lead.

I had another thought: What if the robberies did finance their escapades? It would be possible for this to be the case and for Terry not to have been involved in the holdups.

And an even more disturbing thought crept in; What if Terry knew something? What if he wasn't involved but knew who was, and was keeping quiet because he feared for his family? For Josh, for Marife and Nicole. After all, anyone who would blow up a building and kill 169 people would think nothing about killing two or three more.

Was he being a martyr or was I again being naive?

Terry had told some investigator that he asked McVeigh if he "was going to rob a bank." Where did he get that idea? Did he know McVeigh had robbed banks before?

An unnamed federal official said that Jennifer

McVeigh had given them indications that her brother may have been involved in bank robberies. Maybe that's why she had been granted immunity in exchange for the kind of information that would be brought out at the trial.

The feds must have gotten something from her, because they had set her free, even after it had been reported that she shared her brother's antigovernment feelings, had written rebellious letters to newspapers decrying the storming of Waco, and she was aware that her brother had, years earlier, driven around in a car containing a large bomb.

She must have known he was a nutcase.

It didn't concern me that authorities were investigating Terry's finances. He had made a lot of money selling properties he acquired in our divorce. In one deal, he sold the house and eighty acres of land for $90,000 and kept 40 percent, after the debt was retired. He sold two other pieces of property for $36,000 and $29,000.

I had never kept track of just how much he made. I didn't care. It was his business. But there was no doubt that he was careful with his money. It wouldn't have surprised me to find out he'd buried it in an old coffee can in the yard.

I knew he didn't trust banks. Josh didn't either these days, something I was sure he picked up from his dad. Terry wanted gold and silver because he thought the U.S. monetary system was going to collapse. "It's a house of cards," he had once said. "There's nothing to support it anymore. We just keep printing all this worthless paper."

In the early nineties he and James began using a red-ink stamp on all their currency; the stamp read, DIS-CHARGED WITHOUT PREJUDICE, a suggestion that paper money was not legitimate.

I did find it odd, however, when I read that in 1992 two credit-card companies sued Terry for nearly $40,000. It was very unlike him to run up debts he couldn't pay. To the creditors, the cases were open-and-shut. Terry had used the cards, taken cash advances, and hadn't paid the bills.

But Terry saw it differently.

When First Deposit National Bank sued him in Sanilac County for $13,692 and won a judgment, Terry shouted from the back of the courtroom that the bank's lawyers were "bloodsucking parasites," and also accused the court of being part of a fraudulent scheme. He shouted that the court had no jurisdiction over him.

"He was hollering in a loud voice," Judge Donald Teeple, recalled, "and he refused to step forward. I informed him that if he didn't keep quiet, I'd send him to jail."

It had been a hard year for Terry, and in the court papers he filed in rebuttal to one of the credit-card companies, he mentioned that he had not worked steadily. He also said the government was after him.

Meanwhile, also in 1992, his pal Tim McVeigh was also busy writing. In a letter to his hometown paper in Lockport, New York, he complained about crime, taxes, and "out of control" politicians. The missive ended with the chilling question and warning, "Do we have to shed blood to reform the current system? I hope it doesn't come to that! But it might!"

Terry again appeared in court on January 4, 1993, acting as his own attorney in a lawsuit filed by Chase Manhattan Bank over the unpaid credit-card bills. He based his defense on an argument that what the bank had loaned him was credit, not legal tender, and therefore he did not have to repay the bank with "legal tender," i.e., real money. He sent the bank a homemade "Certified Fractional Reserve" check for $17,861.68 of his own credit as "full payment," in like kind of money.

Months earlier he had filed a court document claiming he had no assets.

This behavior was not that of the Terry Lynn Nichols I had been married to.

After a few days of something of a news blackout, the front pages were again ablaze with stories about the bombing, but two new focal points were Michael Fortier and an obscure robbery that had taken place in Arkansas on November 5, 1994, just a few days before Terry showed up at my house in Las Vegas.

FRIEND OF MCVEIGH IMPLICATES HIM IN BOMBING

FORTIER TO TESTIFY AGAINST MCVEIGH

AND NICHOLS IN PLEA BARGAIN

And the most damning of all:

MCVEIGH FRIEND IMPLICATES NICHOLS

In that story, Fortier claimed he not only knew of Tim McVeigh's plan to blow up the federal building, but was also aware that Terry Nichols would mix the chemicals that would be used in the bombing. However, he said he played no role in the April 19 disaster.

If Fortier had advance knowledge, I couldn't understand how the government could even be contemplating giving him a deal. That was insane. He could have saved the lives of 169 people.

And when he heard about it, Josh kept asking, "How can Michael be walking around free while my dad is in jail? It isn't fair." And he was right.

If, and it was a big if, Fortier knew what was going to happen, he could have prevented it. Now he was going to try to cop out. Either the government had a very weak case or they were making a big mistake in considering a negotiation.

The nation had a right to be incensed.

The *Los Angeles Times* ran a huge picture of Terry's Fort Benning infantry regiment platoon. The photo identified Terry, Michael Fortier, and Tim McVeigh. They had all been there together on June 3, 1988.

Fortier, whom Josh had identified, was admitting that

he had actually cased the federal building with Tim back in December.

That reminded me of the December day Tim had called the house asking if Terry was back from the Philippines. I had just started writing a letter to Terry, unsure if he was dead or alive, and I wondered how Tim knew about the trip.

When I told him about Terry's whereabouts, he said, "That's too bad," sounding a bit hyper. "I really need to talk to him. Do you have a number for him in the Philippines?"

"No, but I have an address," I replied.

"I'll write to him, but I guess I'd better do it in code, because there are a lot of nosy people." I gave him the only address I had for Terry.

I had opened Terry's storage shed only the day before and I was dying to ask Tim what it was all about, and what was going on, but I was honestly afraid. If it was some kind of secret mission I wasn't supposed to know about, he might come and kill me. God, I wanted to know. But I couldn't ask.

When I hung up with Tim, I continued with the letter, hoping and praying that Terry would be alive to receive it. I felt chills run up my arms.

Not until months later did the pieces seem to fall into place. Tim had cased the building with Fortier and could possibly have been looking for someone to drive the get-away car or help with the bomb.

This probably explains why he then called another Kingman pal, one James Rosencrans, who has since told authorities that on the same day McVeigh called me, he called and asked Rosencrans if he wanted to help him by driving a car or truck in a deal he was working on in the Midwest.

I mentioned McVeigh's call in the letter I was writing to Terry, telling him that Tim sounded desperate. I also told him there were a lot of people who loved him and that Josh needed him, and included a Christmas card and a program from Josh's Christmas play. Perhaps, if what he was feeling was just depression, a positive letter might help bring him to his senses.

As I continued reading the paper, I learned that investigators reported that Fortier resembled one of several men who had "cased" a federal building in Omaha several weeks before the Oklahoma City explosion. Witnesses said the men asked specific questions about the Federal Bureau of Alcohol, Tobacco and Firearms offices in the building, including queries about the number of agents and how many were armed.

The other new focal point in the news, the robbery in Arkansas, did not capture my attention immediately, but as I read details of it I began to see how authorities could think it definitely had some connection to McVeigh and maybe to Terry as well.

The victim, Roger Moore, a gun and coin dealer, had stepped out his back door only to be confronted by a man in camouflage gear and a black ski mask. According to the police report, there were probably two assailants. Moore was bound with duct tape and blindfolded while the robbers ransacked his home, stealing cash and goods worth more than $60,000, including seventy guns, silver and gold bars, some precious stones, and an undisclosed number of gold coins.

Although the fifty-nine-year-old Moore could not identify either of the thieves, he did tell police Tim McVeigh had visited him on several occasions and was familiar with his gun collection.

There was the link to McVeigh, aka Tim Tuttle, aka Joe Kyle and who knows what else.

There were never any claims that Terry knew Moore, and Moore failed to identify Terry in a lineup, but the FBI claimed to have found a very damaging tie-in. While searching Terry's house in Herington, agents claimed to have found a safety-deposit-box key belonging to Moore that was stolen in the robbery.

Lawyers will probably be able to explain the key away, but I couldn't. Then again, maybe Tim left it there. He had visited Terry in Herington. The evidence was powerful, but it was still circumstantial. The FBI also noted that in the months following the robbery McVeigh had "wads" of cash and paid cash for everything he did.

I couldn't come up with an explanation for a lot of discrepancies. Why did Terry need aliases, such as Ted Parker and Mike Havens? It wasn't illegal to use an alias, but normal people didn't have any reason to.

When Tim was stopped and arrested the morning of the bombing, he was driving the same yellow Mercury that had supposedly broken down and necessitated his call to Terry asking for a ride. Why would he make a friend drive 480 miles roundtrip from Herington to Oklahoma City if his car could be fixed that easily?

Assuming it was ever really broken in the first place.

And the television set he had brought from Las Vegas. How important was it, really? Sure, Josh watched movies on it the next day, but Terry's house had no antenna and no cable hookup. Odd, but nothing necessarily suspicious. Cable can be ordered, and Terry ordered it on Thursday, the day after the bombing, and an antenna can be erected with little trouble. And as Josh told the FBI, Marife had been nagging his dad about getting a TV.

Another reason some people have a tough time believing the case against Terry is the fact that he spent the morning of April 19 around Herington, picking up business cards, registering his truck with the state, and calling on a couple of local shops, asking about their interest in buying government surplus.

Those are not the actions of a guilty man.

Yet Terry Lynn Nichols sits in an abandoned wing at

El Reno Federal Prison. The public now knows more about his personal life, his small accomplishments, and ultimate failings than a man so private would ever have revealed, yet still he makes no statements. Not even to his loved ones.

Michael Fortier has now made his deal. He'll testify against Terry and McVeigh in exchange for a more lenient sentence and immunity for his wife.

Meanwhile Terry sits and waits, the surveillance cameras recording his every move. The world is still waiting for an explanation, and Josh's question now begs for an answer more than ever: "Why is Michael Fortier out and my dad still in jail?"

12

AFTER WEEKS OF SEARCHING THROUGH DEBRIS
and rubble, tireless rescue workers had unearthed the
bodies of 169 victims of the April 19 bombing that devastated America and blew apart the Alfred P. Murrah
Federal Building in Oklahoma City.

They won't find victim #170.

He lives with me.

In my heart, Joshua Isaac Nichols is both a victim and
a survivor. I could never say to the press that I considered
Josh a victim for fear that my comments would be mis-
construed. Some people would undoubtedly become
indignant, perhaps thinking I was trying to minimize the
grief of the families who lost innocent loved ones in the
deadly blast. Nothing could be further from the truth.

I really don't expect people to understand. After all,
Josh is alive and well. He is thirteen now, and healthy. He
has a future, something those killed in Oklahoma will
never have.

But as his mother, I know he has been robbed of a big
part of his life. His future will never be the same. I wish I
could say this and not sound insensitive, but I'm not sure
how, so I hope I am forgiven by anyone who feels
offended. Those men, women, and children killed in the
Murrah Building will suffer no more. Josh will suffer

every day for as long as he lives. He has been indelibly stamped with a scarlet letter, not one as visible as the adulteress's in the classic novel, but one he will still carry in his heart and soul forever.

He has seen his seventh-grade student yearbook picture on the front page of national newspapers linked forever with John Doe #2.

He has defiantly stood up to the FBI, when, after being questioned and badgered, he said "no more."

He has watched his father being paraded across television screens in handcuffs, wearing shackles and a bullet-proof vest.

He has heard his father referred to as a "babykiller" and one of the cruelest and most inhumane men in the history of America.

He has endured the slings and arrows of the media and cruel people who don't care that he is only a child himself.

He has stood face-to-face with an assistant warden at a maximum-security prison and pleaded to hug his father.

He has been pointed at like an animal in a zoo, laughed at behind his back, and jeered to his face in a mob scene in Oklahoma.

He has been exiled from school as if he were a leper.

He has provided the FBI with key information, and been used by the Bureau to help with clues as if were some robotic databank.

He has lived with James Nichols, Terry Nichols, and Tim McVeigh.

He has stayed at Tim McVeigh's apartment in Lockport, New York, and visited Niagara Falls with his dad and McVeigh.

He knew plea bargainer Michael Fortier from Fort Riley, Kansas, and Kingman, Arizona, and is the person who gave Fortier's name to the FBI.

And he has been pictured on the front page of the

National Enquirer beneath a headline that read: THE BOY WHO COULD SEND THE OKLAHOMA BOMBER TO HIS DEATH.

Tim is a wild driver, Josh told me later. "He almost got us killed on the way to Niagara Falls. He tried to pass a car on a blind hill and there was another car coming from the other direction that he couldn't see. We came so close I was sick. We only missed by about ten feet. Tim just laughed."

Through it all Josh has been strong, and as I reflect on what he has endured, I now have confidence that he will be able to handle whatever life deals him.

The biggest dilemma I faced regarding Josh was whether or not I should agree to let him testify before the grand jury in Oklahoma. In the end I had no choice. The government was insistent that he appear, even going so far as to threaten to subpoena or arrest him as a material witness. Authorities even hinted that he might be served and detained in Oklahoma, while he was there to visit his dad in July.

It was an ongoing battle, and I could certainly see both sides.

First and foremost, I wanted to protect my son. I didn't want him to have to walk into that grand-jury room and face all those jurors and attorneys, even though it would have been a noncombative situation. I knew what it was setting up.

If he testified before the grand jury, he would undoubtedly be called when the regular trial began. And I definitely didn't want him in a courtroom sitting across from Tim McVeigh.

I hated Tim McVeigh, but I was also afraid of him. Afraid that if he hadn't committed the crime alone, his coconspirators might come after me or Josh. I think Josh is also frightened of Tim.

Ever since my testimony before the grand jury in May, there had been speculation and rumor about Josh being called.

To people on the outside, the decision seemed very obvious.

"If the kid knows anything, he should talk. After all, a hundred sixty-nine people had been killed. And if he doesn't know anything about the bombing, so what? What harm could it do?"

Others said, "If he's got nothing to cover up, testifying should be no big deal. America has to come first."

The arguments seemed to make sense, and I was leaning toward agreeing with them, especially after Josh assured me he could handle it. "After all the questions I answered for the FBI, what's a few more?" he said philosophically. "Don't worry, Mom, I'll be all right. I don't really want to testify, but if I have to, no big deal. I'll just tell them the same things I told the FBI. I don't know any more."

Josh felt he had one more thing to offer, and it might prove to be a very strong point in Terry's defense. Most everyone connected with the case agrees that Terry's movements, which the FBI refers to as the "Nichols time line," in the week preceding the bombing are critical to establishing his innocence.

Josh has studied that time line. He has seen inaccuracies in it. He has told the FBI about where his dad was and what his dad did on every day of his visit, demonstrating an amazing ability to recall times, places, and details.

His account of what went on from April 12 to 17 coincides with Terry's, and corroborates what his dad offered as an alibi. That evidence may be the strongest Terry has to offer in his own defense, and may put Josh in the unique position of being his father's salvation.

Few have been willing to believe that Terry was merely a victim of circumstance and misplaced friendship and not one of the most cold-blooded and calculating terrorists in U.S. history.

But Josh stands staunchly by his father.

He has said repeatedly that at no time during his stay in Kansas did he see McVeigh, a Ryder truck, or the mysterious blue barrels. He knew that his dad spoke to McVeigh on the phone a number of times, and that his dad had driven to Oklahoma City to pick Tim up after McVeigh called saying he needed a ride. Tim also promised to give Terry the television set belonging to Josh that he had picked up in Las Vegas.

Terry went. He returned at 2:00 A.M. and he had the television set. Josh could also account for his dad's whereabouts on the other days he spent in Kansas. Most of the time if his dad had an errand to run, Josh tagged along.

On the surface it sounds like an airtight alibi and solid corroboration by a credible eyewitness. But everything, according to the FBI, wasn't that simple. And when they get Josh on the stand, they are sure to ask if he had ever heard his dad or Tim use aliases, and if so, did he find that unusual.

Josh could possibly also defuse all the hullabaloo about knowing how to make a bomb. The statement, on its face, was inflammatory and incriminating. Examined more closely, however, Josh could explain that the reference was to bottle bombs that his dad and uncle taught him to make to blow up unwanted tree stumps on the farm.

But knowing how slick lawyers operate, Josh wouldn't get a chance to elaborate. His words would be taken out of context, and he, like many adults, might become confused by the phrasing of the questions.

And, it would be asked, how could he know what went on the morning after he left, when Terry supposedly lent his pickup to McVeigh for five hours and went to a surplus auction?

The government claims the two men drove Terry's pickup along with the Ryder truck to Geary State Fishing

Lake, an area fifteen miles south of Junction City, Kansas, where they believe the bomb was made. Eyewitnesses say they saw both trucks at Geary Lake, and investigators believe the bomb's fuse was threaded into the cab through holes drilled in the truck.

Josh can't address this matter. And I think he would be carrying the enormous burden of not wanting to say anything that could be harmful to his dad. In his eagerness to help, he might be manipulated into doing just the opposite.

The general public didn't understand that the U.S. attorney and the grand jury didn't need Josh. All the information he had given voluntarily to the FBI during the week we were in custody and the later interviews as contained in reports that were admissible to the grand jury record. He didn't need to repeat it personally. What's more, it was legal for any of the agents who interviewed him in Las Vegas to take the stand at the grand jury and relate what Josh had told them as well as give their interpretation of his accounts.

Attorney Stan Hunterton was adamant about filing a motion to excuse Josh from testifying. Dr. Joan Owen, Josh's counselor, agreed, and she and Stan explained that they felt that forcing Josh to appear in Oklahoma might result in permanent psychological damage. "There may be no way we can prevent him from testifying," Stan explained, "and there's only a slim chance a judge will see it our way, but I think, for the record, you have to file this motion. Besides, it will establish a precedent. If you don't file a motion now, and they want to call Josh at the regular trial, you won't have any grounds to object. They'll say, 'Well, you didn't object to him appearing before the grand jury.'"

We filed a motion in Oklahoma City, asking for the establishment of some sort of parent-child privilege. The judge dismissed our plea without hearing arguments.

There were no cases on record where a child had been granted immunity from testifying against a parent who had committed a capital crime.

Josh would have to testify. The only concession the judge made seemed to be in response to Dr. Owens's affidavit in which she voiced her opinion on the possibility of adverse psychological consequences for Josh.

The judge ordered Josh's testimony be taken in Las Vegas, which reduced the stress level for all of us. Two days later Josh gave his statements and answered questions for two and a half hours without incident in the U.S. attorney's offices in downtown Las Vegas. It was the best we could have hoped for.

One of the key issues the prosecutors wanted to clarify had to do with certain barrels in Terry's garage. There was a discrepancy about their color, whether they were blue or white. Josh had continually read in the paper or heard on the news that the barrels were blue, and he insisted the FBI must have "planted" the barrels if they were blue.

"My friends and I played back there every day," he insisted. "There were no blue barrels. Only white ones."

I think this matter was cleared up to everyone's satisfaction when Josh acquiesced to the possibility that the "blue" barrels he'd been shown in photographs may in reality have been white ones with blue lids. But he wasn't going to back down and agree with the FBI when he was positive the barrels weren't blue.

Josh's life is so different now than it was a year ago, I can hardly point out all the changes.

He's more grown up, but he's also moodier.

At times he'll hear some evidence against Terry presented on TV and he'll get angry and say something like, "Well, I guess things look pretty bad for my dad."

Then, on the next newscast, he'll hear someone or some new item questioning certain evidence and it will give him hope. Or if the bombing is mentioned and

Terry's name doesn't come up in the report, he'll take it as a positive sign.

"If that's true, they might be letting him go, right?"

It depressed him to hear that prosecutors were seeking an extension on the date of their decision about whether to indict Terry. It was not so much the delay that bothered him, but the fact that the new deadline they were asking for was August 11, Josh's birthday. How would you like to celebrate your birthdays for the rest of your life on the day your father was indicted for mass murder?

I've also noticed how Josh's conversation is constantly peppered with references to Tim or his dad. For example, one evening we made a stop at Wal-Mart on Tropicana Avenue and Josh opted to stay in the car and listen to the radio while I ran in to buy a clock. Lee had moved out and taken a lot of little things, as well as some big things like the television. By some stroke of coincidence I bought the exact same clock his dad had purchased on Easter Sunday in Kansas, and Josh said it would bother him every time he looked at it. It would make him think of his dad and that the place Terry was now sleeping had no clocks.

He made me take it back.

He still refuses to eat spaghetti because it was Tim's favorite food, and seeing a Ryder truck always strikes a nerve.

He waits anxiously for Terry's calls, and tries hard to make his dad part of the ongoing events of his life, often talking to him about friends Terry has never met. Once he handed the phone to a friend and introduced him to Terry.

The last time Terry had to appear in court, one of the news stations noted that he was dressed in a sport coat and slacks, in contrast to McVeigh, who appeared in prison clothes. That tidbit did not escape Josh.

"I heard you were all dressed up today, with no place to go," he kidded in his conversation later that night with his dad. "I saw you on TV today. You looked good, except of course for the handcuffs." He tried to make an incredibly awkward situation as normal as possible.

"My dad always did it this way," or "My dad likes peas," or "My dad could fix that," have become regular lines in his conversations. Terry has become bigger than life to him.

Terry had continued sending letters, and at first Josh wrote to him at least once a week, but now he relies on the calls. I urge him to write more, and Terry reminds him how much he appreciates the letters and how much they mean to him, but Josh does not enjoy writing.

Both Josh and I crossed our fingers about school. We were hopeful that the school board and Cannon Middle School would have no objections to him returning as a full-time student.

We had been through a major battle with the school district back in April when everything was so hectic. The school board had advised us that they thought it best if Josh not come back to school for the final two months of the year because it might be too disruptive and too dangerous for other students.

At the time I understood their extra caution. None of us knew what the dangers were. But it also meant that Josh would be home full-time and I had no one to take care of him. To further complicate matters, the school district could not even guarantee a home-study teacher.

"Mrs. Padilla, under the circumstances we are reluctant to put one of our teachers at risk by sending him to your home. We'd don't know if there is any real danger, but we prefer to be cautious at this time."

Eventually they relented and sent a man named Frank Mitchell. Josh's thoughts were obviously on his dad, and the timing for the tutor couldn't have been worse. Mitchell came twice a week at three in the afternoon, just when Josh's friends were getting home from school and he wanted to go out and play. Josh was in no frame of mind to study, and had little incentive. Some teachers might have thrown up their hands, but Mitchell worked through it.

Since Mitchell taught school all day, his time schedule couldn't be changed. Josh toughed it out, and when June came and school was over for regular students, Mitchell came earlier and Josh began to apply himself more diligently.

Things Josh did with his dad have become more important to him as time passes, perhaps because he is afraid he'll never get to do those things again. I think, in his heart, he has prepared himself for the worst while still hoping for the best.

When it was finally announced on August 10 that Terry had been formally indicted for the crime of blowing up the Alfred P. Murrah Federal Building, Josh accepted it with stoic resignation. And when the official word came that the government would definitely seek the death penalty, there was a sadness beyond his years in his eyes. It was as if he himself had been condemned to death.

Since it was generally conceded that Terry was in Kansas at the time of the explosion, a broken boy came out of his room and asked, "If they are found guilty, and it is proven that my dad wasn't there, will he still get the death penalty?"

"Maybe not," I said, my heart not in the answer.

"How long after somebody's convicted before they actually wind up on death row?" he asked, his lips quivering and his eyes holding back tears the way Hoover Dam withstands the Colorado River.

"A long time," I said, putting my arm around him. "But I don't think we should even worry about that now. There's a long way to go yet. Remember, innocent until proven guilty, Josh. And your dad hasn't even been to trial yet.

"You know Mike Tigar is really a tiger. He's a great attorney."

While I was saying these words I remembered a phone conversation I'd had with Terry a month before, one of those calls where he was restricted to twenty minutes. "Don't worry," I'd said. "You have a really good lawyer."

Somberly he replied, "It's going to take more than a good lawyer to get me out of here."

I never told Josh what he said, but I'll never forget his words that day. They haunt me.

The next time I spoke to someone in Stan's office, I asked what the normal length of time was between conviction and the carrying out of the death penalty. The consensus seemed to be about seven or eight years.

That would make Josh twenty or twenty-one if things turned out for the worst. I don't think anything he or I have to say in testimony will swing the pendulum in this case, but I do know the guilt we would feel if we said something to hurt Terry's case, or failed to say something that could help him.

Later in life we would both regret it.

I know already that I will bear the brunt of his rage, and Dr. Owen has warned me that I could lose him. He has to blame someone for what has happened. He can't blame his dad.

He can blame Tim. He can blame me, for divorcing Terry and for revealing those letters. I can only hope that if he rages against me, he will one day see the light. Neither of us is to blame.

No one knew if he would be able to go back to school this year. Whether the district would accept him, whether he would be able to deal with and concentrate on his studies, or if he would want to go back. Then there was the concern about how his peers would relate to him.

In addition, there was always the possibility that he would miss a substantial amount of time if he were called as a witness at the trial. He has said repeatedly that he wants to attend the trial, even asking me if I would rent a house in Oklahoma so we could be there every day to show his dad support and unity.

The school and the school board agreed to let him come back to school. They are at least willing to see how it goes.

Today was his first day of school, as an eighth grader. It was a day he was looking forward to. He has been idle too long. He needs the routine, and as I drove him to school I prayed that he would not encounter any trouble.

At school a couple of kids referred to him jokingly as John Doe. He buried the hurt and let it pass. Someone left a belt buckle with the initials "J. D." on his desk.

He took the bus home from school. It's only a ten-minute ride and it drops him off at the corner of Warm Springs and Spencer, about three blocks from home. As he neared home a boy about his age came running up behind him shouting, "Are you Josh Nichols? Are you Josh Nichols?" Josh said he turned to the boy, a little apprehensive because it was someone he didn't know and because of the way he had run up to him. But realizing he was bigger than the other boy, Josh relaxed.

"Yeah, I'm Josh," he answered, not knowing what to expect.

"My name is John," the boy said coldly. "I'm from Oklahoma. My dad's a fireman in Oklahoma and his station had the windows blown out by the bomb your father set off. I could kill you."

Josh readied for a fight, but the boy just glared at him, then turned and walked away.

Victim #170 was getting a lesson in life.

13

WHERE DO WE GO FROM HERE?

I know I can't answer that. We no longer have normal lives. Every aspect of our being, of our everyday actions, is permeated by what happened on April 19, 1995, and by our unbreakable link to Terry Lynn Nichols.

Much of the evidence against Terry is circumstantial. One day, the hope that he will ever be free again seems absurd. Then, somehow, Josh and I find another ray of hope.

Personally, I want to know the answers. I want to know the truth, the whole truth, and not one person's version.

I don't just have questions for Terry, I have questions for the government. I've learned firsthand that they don't always do things by the book. When necessary, they play hardball, and innocent people can very easily get hurt and become victims left by the wayside.

John Doe #2 was a government mistake. Innocent at first, perhaps, because in their zeal to bring the perpetrators to a swift justice, they erroneously suggested to a grieving nation that another man was with McVeigh when he rented the truck. A $2 million reward and hundreds of thousands of man-hours were committed to finding the elusive "second gunman." It was probably a week before the FBI realized that John Doe #2 did not exist . . .

. . . That David Iniguez, the soldier whom they questioned, and who had, in fact been at the Junction City Ryder rental station in the same time frame, was not affiliated with Tim McVeigh.

They cleared Iniguez but did not bother telling the world that they were virtually certain the search was over.

No bureaucrat wanted to accept responsibility for the wasted manpower and man-hours. Let the wild-goose chase go on for just a little longer, until it eventually faded away on its own.

John Doe #2 was a ghost. A figment of an overzealous agent's imagination.

At this moment a trial seems a long way off.

The lawyers tell us it won't begin before next year.

Josh and I are waiting. That's all we can do. Terry calls once, sometimes twice a week, and it brightens Josh's day whenever he does.

My son does his homework with an eye on the television, which is now on the news channels instead of prime-time shows. He seldom looks at the newspaper, perhaps afraid he'll see his picture on the front page again. Or worse yet, his father's picture.

He hurts when he sees Terry's picture in the paper, because he knows most of the time the text is not flattering. He is still hopeful that his dad will be acquitted and that he will get to spend his Christmas and Easter breaks in Kansas, as well as his summer vacation.

He misses hiking with his dad, camping out, and the things they shared that were special. He doesn't seem angry at the government, but he still carries a lot of anger inside. And right now he doesn't know where to place it.

I can see how he tries to put the whole thing out of

his head, but it is never very far away. A comment, a picture, or a simple act like opening his closet to find one of his dad's army trophies is all it takes to make the tears come.

But when that trial starts, Josh and I are going to be in the eye of the storm once again. Perhaps even more prominently than before.

I don't know if we will be at the trial. It would be expensive, and emotionally draining. I do expect that we will be called upon to testify, and I had a dream, or a nightmare, about that prospect.

In my dream, Josh and I are seated in the hallway outside the courtroom. I am standing, he is seated. I am stroking his hair. I am scheduled to be the next witness for the prosecution. They want me to tell about the letters, to try to explain how Terry might have amassed $20,000 in cash.

They want me to detail what I saw in the Boulder Highway storage shed, to tell them about the masks, the wigs, the camouflage gear. Information so damaging to Terry Nichols it could put a stake in his heart.

My son is begging me not to go in the room. He is holding me so tight I can't move. I have a loyalty to him. I owe him. He is convincing when he says to let them make their case without me.

"I don't want you to be the one to cause my dad to die."

My own tears are cascading down my cheeks, onto my blouse and into his hair. What can I gain? If I go in that room and say what I have to say, the government will not even say thank you, and my son may say good-bye.

I try to reason with him.

"Josh, what I have to say won't be the main evidence. I have to tell the truth. I don't have any way of knowing exactly what it means. Maybe it won't be so damaging."

He is sobbing out loud. Harder than ever.

I gently free myself from his grasp and kiss him on the top of the head again. I squeeze his hand. And I turn to go in the courtroom. Victim #171 is about to be sworn in.

The following is a reproduction
of the actual letter from
Terry Nichols to Lana Padilla.

PICKUP STORAGE

AAAARCO MINI STORAGE

BETWEEN I-95 BRIDGE
& BOULDER STATION
CASINO

TO ENTER LOCKED GATE
        PRESS STAR BUTTON - *
        PRESS CODE BUTTON - 190455
        PRESS POUND BUTTON - #

PICKUP STORAGE IS PAID FOR 2 MONTHS
BEGINNING 22 NOV 94.

→ PICKUP NEEDS REAR BRAKES (SHOES)
        COST ≈ $25.00 FOR SET

'84 GMC 1/2 TON DIESEL PROBABLY TAKES LARGER SET
    (2 3/4" x 11" ?) DO ONE SIDE @ A TIME · EASY TO DO.

OIL HAS BEEN CHANGED @ 4,500 MILES
CHANGE @ EVERY 3,000 MILES QUAKER STATE 10W-40 7 QTS
            PH13 FRAM OIL FILTER

Tim:

IF, SHOULD YOU RECEIVE THIS LETTER THEN CLEAR
EVERYTHING OUT OF CC 37 by 01FEB95 OR PAY TO
KEEP IT LONGER, UNDER TED PARKER OF DECKER. THIS
LETTER HAS BEEN WRITTEN & SEALED BEFORE I LEFT
(21 NOV94) & BEING MAILED BY LANA AS PER MY INSTRUCTIONS
TO HER IN WRITING. THIS IS ALL SHE KNOWS. IT WOULD
BE A GOOD IDEA TO WRITE OR CALL HER TO VERIFY THINGS—

JUST ASK FOR LANA ▮▮▮▮ (CARD ENCLOSED).
YOUR ON YOUR OWN.   GO FER IT!!

  TERRY

  ALSO LIQUIDATE 40

HAVE MY MAIL FORWARDED TO LANA BUT USE MY NAME
AND HER ADDRESS ▮▮▮▮▮▮▮▮▮▮
   MAIL BOXES ETC.

   ▮▮▮▮▮▮▮▮▮▮▮▮

THE PARKER DEAL WAS SIGNED & DATED 07 NOV94 SO YOU
SHOULD HAVE TILL 07 FEB 95 PLUS 5 DAYS GRACE, IF CLOSE
OR THEY DISAGREE THEN SHOULD PAY ANOTHER ▮▮ TERM PERIOD.

AS FAR AS HEAT – NONE THAT I KNOW, THIS LETTER WOULD
BE FOR THE PURPOSE OF MY DEATH.

Items

- EMERGENCY #'s & ADDRESSES
- LETTER TO JENNIFER TO BE MAILED ON 28 JAN 95
- LETTER TO YOU TO BE OPENED AFTER 01 FEB 95
- 2 FILES ON STOCKS
- KEYS

READ AND DO IMMEDIATELY

AN OTHER STORAGE —   AAAABCO MINI STORAGE

RENTED ON 16 NOV 94
PAID FOR 3 MONTHS
TO 16 FEB '95
SPACE # Q106 (DOWN STAIRS)
    SIZE 5'x5'
COMBINATION # 39-21-35 (R·L·R)

ACCESS CODE TO ENTER STORAGE AT GATES —
        PRESS STAR BUTTON ·*
        PRESS CODE BUTTON· 190455
        PRESS POUND BUTTON· #

→ ALL ITEMS IN STORAGE ARE FOR JOSHUA — THE ROUND ITEMS
   ARE HIS WHEN HE TURNS AGE 21, ALL ELSE NOW.
   PICKUP CAN BE SOLD, BUT MONEY FROM PICKUP PUT AWAY
   FOR JOSH TO BUY HIS OWN VEHICLE.

→ OTHER STORAGE — LOCATED IN KITCHEN BEHIND UTINSEL
   DRAWER BETWEEN DISHWASHER & STOVE. REMOVE DRAWER
   (THERE ARE 2 SMALL LEVERS - ONE ON EACH SIDE OF DRAWER ON RAIL -
   PULL DRAWER OUT TILL IT STOPS THEN FLIP LEVELS DOWN & PULL
   DRAWER COMPLETELY OUT) THEN LOOK ALL THE WAY BACK INSIDE.
   TAKE AND PUSH HARD AGAINST BACK PANEL (BOTH SIDES & BOTTOM
   ARE GLUED, TOP NOT) AFTER IT'S BROKE FREE, REMOVE WOOD PANEL
   THEN REMOVE PLASTIC BAG. ALL ITEMS IN PLASTIC BAG ARE TO
   BE SENT TO MARIFE FOR NICOLE IF FOR ANY REASON MY LIFE
   INSURANCE DOESN'T PAY MARIFE, OTHERWISE ½ GOES TO
   MARIFE AND ½ TO JOSHUA.
                        OVER

MARIFE WILL KNOW WHAT IS AT STORAGE & HOME.

AS OF NOW-ONLY MARIFE, YOU, & MYSELF KNOW WHAT
THERE IS AND WHERE IT IS. I HOPE YOU WILL DO AS
I HAVE STATED. JOSH HAS JUST A FEW YEARS BEFORE
HE'S CAPABLE OF BEING ON HIS OWN AND MARIFE & NICOLE
HAVE MANY MORE YEARS OF SUPPORT NEEDED.
THERE IS NO NEED TO TELL ANYONE ABOUT THE ITEMS
IN STORAGE & AT HOME. AGAIN ONLY THE THREE (3) OF US
WILL KNOW. I HAVE THE MOST TRUST IN YOU HERE
IN THE U.S. TO DO AS I HAVE WRITTEN. IT WOULD
PROBABLY BE BEST TO WIRE THE ITEMS TO MARIFE, 3 M AT
A TIME OVER 2-3 MONTHS.

YOU WILL HAVE TO CONTACT TIM TO GET THE TITLE FOR THE
PICKUP, HE SHOULD KNOW WHERE IT'S AT. WRITE TO HIS SISTER —

████████████████████████████████████

YOU CAN TELL JOSH AFTER YOU FINISH WITH ALL
THE DETAILS.

THERE ARE TWO (2) STOCK POWER OF ATTYS. IN THE STOCK FILE
SIGNED BUT NOT FILLED OUT. YOU SHOULD BE ABLE TO TAKE
CARE OF THEM W/ THE STOCK POWER OF ATTYS.